FROM
STARTUP
TO
EXIT

SHIRISH NADKARNI

FROM STARTUP TO EXIT

An Insider's Guide to Launching and Scaling Your Tech Business

HarperCollins
LEADERSHIP

An Imprint of HarperCollins

To my family—Rohit, Priyanka, and Shreya,
Hope you get to follow your own entrepreneurial
journey and achieve great success!

To my wife, Mona,
Thanks for being my best friend and partner in life.

Published by HarperCollins Leadership, an imprint of HarperCollins Focus LLC.

Any internet addresses, phone numbers, or company or product information printed in this book are offered as a resource and are not intended in any way to be or to imply an endorsement by HarperCollins Leadership, nor does HarperCollins Leadership vouch for the existence, content, or services of these sites, phone numbers, companies, or products beyond the life of this book.

ISBN 978-1-4002-2535-4 (eBook)
ISBN 978-1-4002-2534-7 (PBK)

Library of Congress Control Number: 2021938402

Printed in the United States of America
21 22 23 24 25 LSC 10 9 8 7 6 5 4 3 2 1

CONTENTS

PART II: COMPANY FORMATION

PART IV: RUNNING YOUR COMPANY

PREFACE

IN 1999, WHEN I DECIDED to leave Microsoft to start my first company, TeamOn, it seemed like a daunting task. I had an idea for the company I wanted to build, but I had no cofounder. While I was in the middle of the dot-com boom, the internet was still immature and there were very few resources available to educate a first-time founder. I recall that I found a book that explained the venture capital ecosystem and the fundamentals of fundraising and term sheets. However, the book didn't cover the basics of idea validation, achieving product/market fit, or how to develop a go-to-market strategy, all essential concepts to building a successful company.

I struggled to get the company off the ground initially. After many months of searching for a cofounder with the right technical expertise, I recruited my eventual cofounder, Shaibal Roy, in the San Francisco Bay Area. Shaibal was intrigued by my idea but was not willing to leave his company and relocate to Seattle where I was based. We finally agreed that he would work part-time on my startup until I successfully raised a Series A round. Fortunately, we were at the height of the dot-com bubble at that time, and I raised a $15 million round to fund the company. As you will read later in this book, the original idea didn't work out, and I had to pivot the company before we found success through an eventual acquisition by BlackBerry.

It's been twenty years since the start of my entrepreneurial journey. I am surprised that there have been very few good books written in the meantime covering a founder's journey all the way from ideation to exit. *Venture Deals*,[1] a classic written by famed investor Brad Feld, explains the venture capital world and the details of fundraising and negotiating a term sheet. *Hot Seat: The Startup CEO Guidebook*,[2] written by Dan Shapiro, another Seattle-based serial entrepreneur, is a personal favorite. He details his learnings founding and running multiple startups. Still, as I advised many founders, I felt that founders could benefit from having a "virtual" seasoned advisor at their side who could guide them along the entire journey in all aspects of company building.

My initial venture in helping startup founders began with the founding of the TiE Entrepreneur Institute in Seattle in 2018. TiE is a global nonprofit focused on fostering entrepreneurship with more than sixty chapters all over the world. I have served as president of the TiE Seattle chapter and have been on the board for the last five years. The TiE Entrepreneur Institute was organized into three modules with fifteen different sessions covering a variety of topics, including company formation, ideation, fundraising, and go-to-market strategy. The sessions were conducted by experienced entrepreneurs, venture capitalists (VCs), and lawyers along with a fireside chat with successful entrepreneurs. The TiE Entrepreneur Institute was very well received and has now been conducted over Zoom for all TiE chapters around the world.

In 2019, to spread the word further, I started writing a series of blog articles on LinkedIn and Medium covering many of the same topics as the TiE Entrepreneur Institute. By happenstance that year, I met a former Microsoft colleague, Kumar Mehta, who is the author of *The Innovation Biome*. When Kumar heard of my blog articles, he encouraged me to convert them into a book. Coincidently at that time, HarperCollins had entered into a relationship with the Microsoft Alumni Network to publish books written by Microsoft alumni. I contacted HarperCollins and reached an agreement with them to publish this book under the Microsoft Alumni Network imprint. My vision for the book is to cover all aspects of an entrepreneur's journey—from ideation, company formation, fundraising, and scaling the company to eventually achieving an exit.

The book is organized into five sections.

In "Part I: Ideation," I discuss what makes a good idea for a startup. I outline the strategic considerations to determine the viability of an idea. For example, a platform shift is an ideal time to disrupt incumbents, as companies like Amazon and Netflix have shown. I discuss the process for finding product/market fit and how to go about executing a pivot if your original idea is not getting traction.

In "Part II: Company Formation," I discuss the fundamentals of forming a company. I outline the various options, which include S corporation, LLC (limited liability company), and C corporation, and the pros and cons of each. I discuss the thorny issue of splitting up founder equity, which can be tricky given that each founder brings different capabilities and contributions to the table. Next, I explain the concept of cap (capitalization) tables and how the equity is split up among founders, investors, and employees. I provide an example of a financing to explain how the cap table changes as you go through various financing rounds. Finally, I explain the concept of startup options and the difference between incentive stock options (ISOs) and non-qualified stock options (NSOs).

In "Part III: Fundraising," I discuss the various sources for raising funding at different stages of your company. I outline different types of funding vehicles, such as convertible debt, SAFEs, Series Seed, venture debt, crowdfunding, and the pros and cons of each. I explain the meaning of various terms in a term sheet for raising a preferred round of equity financing. It is important that you understand all these terms in order to properly negotiate a term sheet with your VC investor. Finally, I discuss how to build a compelling investor pitch and provide you with a detailed outline for an investor presentation.

In "Part IV: Running Your Company," I discuss various aspects of growing and managing your company, including hiring great employees, building a vibrant company culture, and becoming a great leader. I outline different options to develop a sound business model for your company. I explain the core concepts of unit economics so you understand how to balance your cost of acquiring your customers against the lifetime value that you generate from them. Finally, given the major downturns that we experience every decade or so, this section outlines how CEOs should manage their companies through deep recessions and emerge in one piece at the end of it.

In "Part V: Finding an Exit," I describe the two options for finding an exit for your company—through an acquisition or through an IPO (initial public offering). I discuss how you should prepare your company for an acquisition even though you may not be looking for one in the short term. I explain the importance of hiring an investment bank so you can streamline the process for the acquisition and get multiple acquirers to the table. If you are one of the few companies lucky enough to get to an IPO, there's a lot of preparation to be done. The book outlines the three ways that a company has to go public—to do a traditional IPO, to do a direct listing or to merge with a SPAC (Special Purpose Acquisition Company). The book explains in detail the preparatory work that needs to be done regardless of the option that you decide to pursue.

The journey from ideation to founding to an exit is a long and arduous one that very few entrepreneurs successfully make. The goal of this book is to be your guidebook through this journey, providing you with insights and tips to successfully navigate your way to a meaningful exit. I have shared many of the important lessons that I have learned through three different startups, raising more than $30 million in funding, and achieving two successful exits. It is the book that I wish I had when I started my first company twenty years ago. I hope that many of you who are aspiring entrepreneurs will be motivated to begin this journey. It doesn't take a special breed to become successful entrepreneurs.

Good luck and all the best in building your business!

PART I

IDEATION

HOW GOOD
IS YOUR IDEA?

The TeamOn Story

In 1997, at the height of the dot-com boom, I was put in charge of product planning for MSN.com (Microsoft Network). MSN was in a full-fledged transition from a proprietary online service like AOL to an open web-based portal called MSN.com. We were behind other leading portals such as Yahoo, Excite, and others. We were determined to catch up by leveraging Microsoft's cash hoard to acquire companies offering essential internet-based services. One critical service we felt was important for us to provide was email.

In our research, we came across free web-based email services like Hotmail and RocketMail. While most people at that time got email through internet service providers (ISPs), Hotmail disrupted the market by offering a first-of-its-kind application as a web-based service. It was free and, unlike ISP email, it allowed you to access your email from any internet-connected computer with a simple web-based interface.

Hotmail was a simple but brilliant idea. After its launch in 1996, Hotmail started growing like a weed, adding more than one million users per month by 1997. It didn't take us very long to decide that Microsoft needed to acquire Hotmail. The acquisition was expensive—almost $400 million—but well worth it as it drove significant growth for the MSN platform.

In the summer of 1998, after doing the initial work to integrate Hotmail into the MSN platform, I decided to take a sabbatical from Microsoft to contemplate my next move. We were in the middle of the dot-com boom as we had never seen before. Companies were raising $15 to $25 million in Series A funding with just beta products and no proof of market adoption. I had spent more than a decade at Microsoft and decided to try my luck at doing my own startup. I wanted to find out if I had the chops to make it on my own without the backing of a company like Microsoft.

Email was my passion. Even before the Hotmail acquisition, I was the product manager responsible for launching Microsoft Mail on the Mac and PC platforms in the early nineties. In the mid-nineties, Microsoft launched a client server solution for corporate email and scheduling called Microsoft Exchange. However, Microsoft Exchange was designed for large enterprises that could afford to hire system administrators to manage their server farm. It was much too complicated for small businesses that couldn't afford their own IT staff.

Seeing the success of Hotmail, it dawned on me to offer an enterprise-grade email and scheduling service for small businesses that was completely web-based. Small businesses would no longer have to purchase servers, hire IT staff, back-up email, and deal with upgrades and bug fixes as they did with Microsoft Exchange. Our web-based service, which we named TeamOn, launched in 1999 and was one of the first SaaS (Software as a Service) solutions at that time. Salesforce, which popularized the term "SaaS," launched that same year.

Like Hotmail, TeamOn was a good idea in concept. Unfortunately, it was ahead of its time when we launched the service. Although we signed up hundreds of thousands of users, usage was low and conversion to our paid offering was poor. Penetration of broadband internet access was low among small businesses, which made it challenging to use a web-based email solution. Users also didn't care much about group calendaring/scheduling services as most people didn't use a digital calendar at that time. Finally, the concept of Software as a Service was relatively new at that time, and most businesses were uncomfortable moving their corporate information to a public cloud. Almost a decade later, as broadband internet became ubiquitous and SaaS applications became more prevalent, Gmail and Office 365 would prove the need for a solution like TeamOn. With the failure of the original TeamOn concept, we were forced to pivot to a mobile email solution that eventually got significant traction. More on this a little later.

The Birth of Livemocha

Fast forward to 2005. I was traveling on vacation with my family. We had just landed in Spain late in the evening. We rented a car at the airport and headed to our hotel. Unfortunately, we didn't have GPS in our rental car, and we had to rely on printed maps to navigate our way to the hotel. It was dark, and soon enough we got lost. We found our way to the closest gas station to ask for directions. Unfortunately, no one spoke English, and we couldn't understand the directions that we were getting from the locals. I turned to my teenage kids for help as they had studied Spanish for several years in school. Alas, all I got were blank stares—I discovered that they had almost no conversational abilities in Spanish. Fortunately, an

English-speaking person soon pulled up to the gas station, and we finally got the directions we needed. This incident reinforced in my mind the importance of conversational practice to properly learn a language.

The following year, one of my cofounders, Raghav Kher, noticed for the first time kiosks at the airport with bright yellow boxes promoting language learning through a CD-ROM-based software package called Rosetta Stone. Rosetta Stone promised that you could learn a language just like a child by simply watching a series of pictures with audio and text in a foreign language. Rosetta Stone invested heavily in marketing not just with kiosks but also with expensive TV advertising. Raghav purchased a copy of Rosetta Stone to learn Spanish but was struck by the fact that, in the day and age of broadband internet, Rosetta Stone was still selling CD-ROM-based software. It occurred to him that there might be a real opportunity to disrupt Rosetta Stone with an internet-based learning solution.

Growing up in India, I learned six different languages, including English. I knew that the only way to really pick up a new language was through intense conversational practice with native language speakers. This is the reason that my kids had not developed any conversational proficiency in Spanish. The textbook-focused approach that they took in school didn't provide them with enough conversational practice to become proficient. I was excited by Raghav's insight and agreed that the time was ripe to introduce a whole new approach to language learning that combined language instruction with the ability to practice conversational skills with native speakers. Globalization was happening rapidly, creating the demand to learn English all over the world. Not only was internet penetration increasing rapidly, but more and more internet users were gaining broadband access, enabling the delivery of high-quality learning content. Finally, Facebook was gaining increasing popularity, making it possible to create private social networks or communities based on common interests like language learning.

Raghav, Krishnan Seshadrinathan, and I decided to take the plunge into language learning, and Livemocha was launched in September 2007. Our vision was to provide language instruction combined with a social network of native speakers that would help learners develop conversational language proficiency. Each language learner was both student and teacher. A native English speaker learning Spanish could help a Chinese-language learner speak English. In turn, the native English speaker would get help learning Spanish from a native Spanish speaker from Latin America. Livemocha took off like a rocket because people loved the idea of seeking help from native speakers. We had a hundred thousand registered users in three months and a million within a year. Over the next four years, Livemocha grew rapidly to more than 15 million registered users in more than two hundred countries before being acquired by Rosetta Stone in 2012.

Unlike TeamOn, Livemocha addressed the real and immediate need of people all around the world to learn English. English-language proficiency can make a world of difference to people's lives, giving them access, among other things, to better paying jobs. Livemocha, in particular, was successful because users were looking for a solution that gave them access to native speakers, which they knew was essential to developing proper conversational proficiency.

What Makes a Great Startup Idea?

You think you have come up with a brilliant idea for your startup. You have spoken to your friends and colleagues, and they think that the idea has merit. You have even done the preliminary market research and spoken to many potential customers, and feedback has been positive. But how do you really know that it will form the basis for a great company? Figuring this out is no easy task. After all, VCs are paid millions of dollars in management fees, and even then, for the most successful investors, only one out of ten picks is a major hit. To consider whether a startup idea has the potential to become a hit, it is important to consider the idea from a number of different strategic perspectives discussed below.

INCUMBENTS ARE HARD TO BEAT ON THEIR OWN TURF

Most markets you will target have existing players and market leaders that have been around for years. Incumbents are extremely hard to beat unless there is a major transformation in the industry that you can exploit first. Incumbents typically have a strong industry reputation, a host of features, a fine-tuned sales engine, and customer lock-ins that make it difficult for customers to consider a new player in the market.

Everyone today is familiar with the success of Microsoft Office. What people don't know is how difficult it was for Microsoft to gain a leadership position in the office productivity space before Windows became a popular platform. Before the advent of Windows, WordPerfect and Lotus 1-2-3 were the de facto market leaders on the MS-DOS operating system. Microsoft had its own MS-DOS-based offerings called Microsoft Word and Microsoft Multiplan. However, Microsoft had very little success beating WordPerfect and Lotus 1-2-3. Users were just too used to the keystroke-based user interfaces of WordPerfect and Lotus 1-2-3 and were locked into the macros that they created in Lotus 1-2-3.

Once Windows 3.0 came on the scene in 1990 and started becoming popular, things shifted in Microsoft's favor. WordPerfect and Lotus made the mistake of simply porting their applications from MS-DOS to Windows, which meant that the applications didn't perform well on Windows. Not surprisingly, Microsoft built new word processing and spreadsheet apps from the ground up that were designed to take advantage of the capabilities offered by Windows. Next, Microsoft made the brilliant move to package these applications along with Microsoft PowerPoint into a bundle called

Microsoft Office and made it cheaper than purchasing each application individually. Over time, Microsoft made sure that all the applications had consistent user interfaces and that it was easy to share data across these applications. It was no surprise that, as Windows became more popular, the market share leadership shifted to Microsoft Office as users wanted the best and most comprehensive suite of applications for Windows.

GLOBAL INDUSTRY TRANSFORMATIONS

The best opportunities for disruption happen when the industry you are targeting is undergoing a dramatic transformation. At that time, incumbents are typically slow to move because they have existing investments and business models that they are unwilling to disrupt. Microsoft, for example, failed to recognize how its hold on the PC industry would be disrupted first by the internet and later by mobile devices. It took a very expensive acquisition of Hotmail for Microsoft to get into the game with MSN.com, and it was soon eclipsed again by major players like Google and Facebook. On the mobile front, Microsoft invested initially in its Pocket PC platform but failed to see the shift to mobile by early players like Research In Motion (RIM) with its iconic BlackBerry device. Later, Apple and Android completely upended the mobile market with their touch-based interfaces and application platforms. By the time that Windows mobile came on the scene, it was too late for Microsoft, and it never got beyond a 1 to 2 percent market share in the mobile market.

With TeamOn, my plan was to ride the wave of SaaS applications with the shift from IT-installed on-prem (on premises) solutions to applications that operated in the cloud. In the 2000 time frame, when broadband internet was becoming more widespread among business users, SaaS-based applications provided performance similar to that of locally installed client server applications. SaaS-based applications offered numerous benefits over on-prem applications— companies didn't have to hire an expensive IT staff to install and upgrade the applications and back up user data. It was also possible to access applications from any location with internet access—users were not limited to accessing an application only from within a corporate network.

When Livemocha was launched, the entire world was going through a globalization phenomenon with dramatic outsourcing of manufacturing and knowledge worker jobs. Global trade was also showing significant growth as tariffs and trade barriers were coming down. Worldwide travel between various regions was increasing significantly as employees at multinational corporations had to travel internationally to coordinate their activities with their employees, customers, and vendors. These transformations were all responsible for the significant interest in foreign language learning, especially English, throughout the world.

While the trend toward globalization was accelerating, a number of social networks began emerging and capturing end user attention. Facebook and Twitter launched in the early 2000 time frame, popularizing the notion of social networking. As a result, people started feeling more comfortable interacting with other like-minded people on the internet. A number of special community-focused social networks also emerged to leverage the trend toward social networking.

With Livemocha, we decided to disrupt the traditional CD-ROM-based learning model popularized by Rosetta Stone by offering a web-based social language-learning tool. Unlike Rosetta Stone, the offering was initially free. Later, we introduced a premium version that offered a more advanced set of learning courses with conversational video and grammar content. It took a long time for Rosetta Stone to respond to Livemocha as it was wedded to the traditional CD-ROM model, which sold at a high price backed by expensive TV advertising. Because it was a public company, it was on the hook to meet quarterly goals and didn't have the luxury of making a freemium offering like Livemocha.

• • •

LOOKING AHEAD, the COVID-19 crisis is creating another global transformation in the way we work together, how commerce is conducted, and how experiences are delivered. In a matter of weeks, companies with white-collar office workers were forced to an all remote work situation. Use of virtual collaboration tools like Zoom accelerated dramatically and companies found that employees can be equally productive working from home. The use of workplace automation and collaboration tools like Slack, Microsoft Teams, Smartsheet, Asana, and others also increased significantly. As a result, many companies like Twitter and Zillow indicated that they will let their workers work remotely on an indefinite basis. Given the prevalence of remote work, I fully expect that new collaboration tools will emerge that will allow employees to be more productive working from home.

As the COVID-19 crisis has dampened consumer demand, many companies have also experienced significant impact to their revenues. There is, therefore, significant pressure on companies to correspondingly reduce their expenses and make their workforces more efficient. As a result, there's increased interest in digital transformation as a way for companies to create "Digital First" work from anywhere experiences with increased automation. Companies like UIPath, which provide tools for robotic process automation (RPA), have seen dramatic increase in sales as RPA has become a key tool to reduce costs involved in repetitive office tasks.

Retail commerce is another area that is being disrupted because of the COVID-19 crisis. There has been a dramatic shift from physical retail sales to online e-commerce as shoppers are cautious about shopping at malls. Demand for delivery services like Instacart and DoorDash has also exploded. These changes are going to create new opportunities for startups to deliver innovative products that satisfy the need for people to conduct commerce online as opposed to in person. A number of online-first consumer brands like Warby Parker, Allbirds, and Madison Reed have emerged in the last few years and have successfully captured consumers' imagination. I expect that the category of online-only consumer brands will explode as people become more comfortable consummating their purchases online.

TECHNOLOGY PLATFORM SHIFTS

Over the last three decades, we have seen new technology platforms emerge that have created tremendous opportunities for startups. We had the emergence of the PC platform in the eighties, followed by the internet platform in the nineties. Finally, mobile emerged as the broadest platform for computing in the early 2000s, enabling more than 4.5 billion users worldwide to gain access to the internet.

Each of these new technology platforms has allowed a whole new generation of companies to emerge and become massive players in the industry. Microsoft rode the PC platform wave, followed by Google and Amazon, which rode the internet wave, and, finally, Facebook and Apple rode the move to mobile. A number of new companies emerged that disrupted existing market leaders that did not adapt fast enough to the emerging new platforms. Amazon disrupted Barnes & Noble before becoming a general purpose e-commerce platform. Netflix disrupted Blockbuster, and now it is disrupting traditional cable companies, which are losing subscribers by the millions as they cut the cord. In fact, neither of my adult kids has a cable TV subscription. Instead, they rely on Netflix, Amazon Prime, and Hulu to access made-for-TV content.

Over the last few years, we are seeing a significant opportunity for new startup creation with the emergence of artificial intelligence and machine learning (AI/ML) technology. The advent of cheap GPU-based computing power and AI/ML services offered by all the major cloud providers like Amazon Web Services, Microsoft Azure, and Google Cloud Platform has enabled a whole new generation of AI/ML-based startups to emerge and disrupt existing players in their market. Startups need access to a large amount of labelled data to build machine learning models that make useful predictions for specific use cases. The most successful startups are the ones that have gained early access to proprietary data that they can utilize to fine-tune their models.

KenSci is a Seattle-based company that is leveraging AI/ML technology in the healthcare space. The company was started by Dr. Ankur Teredesai, a computer science professor at the University of Washington, and Samir Manjure, the company's CEO. KenSci's risk prediction platform for healthcare is engineered to ingest, transform, and integrate disparate sources of healthcare data, including EHR, claims, admin/finance, and streaming. KenSci uses machine learning to recognize patterns in large volumes of data, helping healthcare systems view the granular details of the patient's history and predict future risks for optimal care. For example, KenSci makes risk of readmission and end of life predictions to help healthcare providers avoid adverse changes in their patients' health.

NETWORK EFFECTS

According to Wikipedia, "A network effect (also called network externality or demand-side economies of scale) is the effect described in economics and business that an additional user of a good or service has on the value of that product to others. When a network effect is present, the value of a product or service increases according to the number of others using it." We have seen many examples of how powerful network effects can be in creating unstoppable, winner-take-all juggernauts. eBay was an early example in the auctions market. Many later entrants like Yahoo failed to take on eBay because of the network effect it had established. Facebook and Airbnb are more recent examples where the value of the network has grown exponentially as more users joined their network. In my case, with Livemocha, we saw our social networking capabilities create network effects that powered our growth to 15 million members in only a matter of a few years. As a result of our powerful network effects, we saw virtually no competitors that adopted our approach to language learning.

As you think through your idea, it will be useful to think about opportunities to create network effects as we did with Livemocha. Marketplaces and social networking apps are typically natural candidates for creating network effects. However, even enterprise apps have the potential for creating network effects. Slack is a good example of a solution that has a network effect as more users get on to its platform within a large corporate environment. App Annie is another example of a solution that has created a network effect since it offers benchmarking features for app developers. As more apps utilize App Annie to track their usage, App Annie can provide more data on how an app compares with other apps in the same category.

Network effects are not insurmountable, as Facebook has seen. It was disrupted first by Instagram, which offered filters for photo sharing, and later by Snapchat, which offered the concept of ephemeral messaging to win the minds and hearts of teenagers. Fortunately, Facebook acquired Instagram as well as WhatsApp but failed in its effort to acquire Snapchat. Once you become an established player, you have to be on the lookout for young, hungry startups that are looking to disrupt you.

VIRALITY

The term *viral marketing* was invented by Tim Draper, general partner at Draper Fisher Jurvetson, in the context of Hotmail. Tim introduced the idea by asking the Hotmail team to add a signature "Get your free email at Hotmail" to every email that a Hotmail user sent out. It was responsible for the dramatic growth of Hotmail following its launch in 1996. Hotmail's rapid growth was one of the key reasons that Microsoft decided to acquire Hotmail in 1997.

Having a viral aspect to your application can dramatically reduce your overall cost of acquisition and drive rapid customer growth. It can be even more effective if your application is inherently viral. By "inherently viral," I mean an application that causes its users to actively recruit other users. Hotmail was not an inherently viral application. It got free advertising every time someone sent out an email from a Hotmail account. However, the recipient didn't need to have Hotmail installed in order to receive email from a sender using Hotmail. Skype, on the other hand, was an inherently viral application because both parties to a Skype call have to be on Skype to make the call. As a result, an initiator of a Skype call is likely to recruit the other party to use Skype. However, virality can die off because of technology changes. Skype, for example, has been displaced by WhatsApp, which originally started as a text messaging app. Since introducing video calling features in 2016, WhatsApp has become the de facto audio/video calling app for consumers all over the world.

Enterprise applications can also have viral characteristics. Slack is a great example of a viral application. Its users are motivated to recruit other users so that everyone can communicate easily using Slack. As you think about your startup idea, make sure to think about whether you have an inherently viral application or if you can include viral elements in it. Introducing virality will make it much more possible for your idea to become successful and reduce your overall cost for customer acquisition.

ASPIRINS, NOT VITAMINS

Once you have evaluated your idea from a strategic perspective using the attributes discussed above, it is important to understand how big a pain point you are addressing. As most VCs would say, they are looking to fund aspirins, not vitamins. Ideally, you are addressing a pounding headache where customers are knocking down your door to gain access to your solution. In addition, make sure that your solution is materially better than existing solutions in the market.

Slack is a great example of an "aspirin" solution that addressed the big problem caused by email overload that was destroying productivity for employees, especially in large enterprises. An email inbox is a serial list of communications of all kinds that a person has to wade through to find and act on email messages that are directly relevant to their work. Unlike email, which is a one-to-many communication channel, Slack has a team-oriented communication architecture. With Slack, you can set up channels for specific projects. Communication and updates relevant to these projects can be routed into specific channels that team members can browse at their convenience. This can significantly reduce the communication that would normally go over email, thus allowing the use of email for more direct one-to-one communication.

Slack also makes it easy to have real-time conversations with any teammate. With direct messaging, it's easy to grab someone's attention when you need a quick response. Slack has made it very simple for corporations large and small to adopt its solution by making it free to get started. Slack was a dramatic improvement over email, which contributed to its rapid growth into a multibillion-dollar company.

In the consumer space, Livemocha was successful because it addressed the pressing need of people all around the world to learn English. In most developing countries, strong English-language proficiency can make a big difference in people's livelihood, allowing them to gain access to better paying jobs. Language education in brick-and-mortar schools can be quite expensive in these countries, which created the demand for inexpensive language-learning tools over the internet. In addition, most English-language learners didn't have access to native English speakers to develop English speaking proficiency. Livemocha became very popular because language learners could connect with native English speakers and improve their English speaking skills. In addition, like Slack, Livemocha was free to get started, and consumers had to pay only to gain access to video and grammar content and certified tutors on its platform.

ACHIEVING PRODUCT/MARKET FIT

The term *product/market fit* was originally popularized by Andy Rachleff, the cofounder of Benchmark Capital. According to Marc Andreessen, "Product/market fit means being in a good market with a product that can satisfy the market."[1] For a startup to succeed, achieving product/market fit is absolutely critical. It is a lot easier to achieve product/market fit if your company is riding a major technology shift or a global industry transformation that is creating new market opportunities or providing new ways to deliver a superior solution.

It is often easy to mistake growth in customers for product/market fit. Growth is easy to buy, especially if you are lucky enough to raise a boatload of money on the basis of your reputation and idea. What is critical to sustainable growth is driving real customer engagement and retention. Without customer engagement and retention, your growth will dry up the moment you turn off your customer acquisition spigot. With real product/market fit, you will see material customer growth without spending significant marketing dollars because word of mouth for your product is powerful.

BranchOut was a professional networking product that launched in 2011 on the Facebook platform. At that time, it was possible for an app to leverage Facebook's social graph to spam a user's friends. On the basis of this capability, BranchOut grew to more than 30 million users and raised $50 million in funding. However, it had no real engagement and retention, and once Facebook shut off access to the social graph, its user growth lost steam, leading to an ignominious ending.

Example of Great Product/Market Fit

BlackBerry is a great example of a product that achieved amazing product/market fit from the outset. Conversely, its competitor, the Palm VII, which was a market leader in the PDA (personal digital assistant) category, failed to achieve product/market fit as a mobile PDA. Unlike the Palm VII, the original RIM 950 device, which launched in 1999, was initially designed to be primarily an email-focused device and not a full-fledged PDA. The RIM device addressed a real pain point—the difficulty business users faced when accessing their email on the road. There was no Wi-Fi or internet connectivity at airports at that time; you had to wait until you got to a hotel to connect your laptop to a phone and dial into your corporate network.

The critical capabilities offered by the RIM device included:

- End-to-end encryption for your corporate email. This was a critical feature to get corporate users on board.

- Push email. Email just showed up magically on your device. This completely obscured the fact that the device was working a very slow mobile network.
- Thumb-style keyboard made it possible to type out fairly long email responses.
- Amazing battery life that allowed the device to work for days on a single charge.

The Palm VII, on the other hand, offered none of these capabilities. You couldn't sync your device with your corporate email account. It required the use of a stylus to compose email. Its main focus instead was a weak web "clippings" service that attempted to offer condensed content given that generalized web browsing was really not possible on the slow network on which it operated. BlackBerry took the lead in 2000, outselling the Palm VII by 40 percent, and never looked back until its demise at the hands of the iPhone.

The BlackBerry device nailed the key use case for the user, which was mobile email access to existing email accounts. It focused its design on creating a great user experience even if it meant that the device didn't offer other features like a web browser. These capabilities were added at a much later stage when devices and mobile networks could support these capabilities.

What Does Product/Market Fit Look Like?

You will know when you have achieved product/market fit. Customers will return your calls, your sales cycle will be short, the press will be contacting you to write about your hot product, and, most important, customer engagement and retention will be high. However, to be more specific, there are metrics you can track that will let you know whether you are achieving strong momentum with your product.

According to Andrew Chen, a well-known blogger, these are the metrics that you need to hit if you are a consumer product:

- Usage three out of every seven days
- Organic growth of hundreds of sign-ups/day
- Thirty percent of users are active the day after sign-up
- Clear path to one hundred thousand users

If you are an Enterprise SaaS product, these are the metrics that you need to hit:

- Five percent conversion rate from free-to-paid
- 3X LTV (lifetime value) to CAC (customer acquisition cost) ratio
- Less than 2 percent monthly churn
- Clear path to $100,000 MRR (monthly recurring revenue)

Initial Concept Testing

Before launching your MVP (minimum viable product), I strongly encourage you to engage in testing your concept. Madrona Venture Labs, a Seattle-based incubator, tests out dozens of ideas a year through a multitude of techniques outlined below.

- *Customer interviews:* You should interview potential customers from the market segments that you are targeting. If possible, use a neutral interviewer so you don't ask leading questions that give you the answers you are looking for. Look to do about thirty to fifty interviews. In the interview, don't go right to your solution. Instead, start by asking what are the top three problems the customer is facing. If the customer's list does not include the problem you are addressing, that should be a strong warning sign to you. Next, ask the customer about the problem you are addressing and if he or she views it as a problem. Ask where the problem is ranked, how it is currently being addressed, and what is the customer's level of satisfaction with the current solution. Ideally, you want to be addressing a top three problem for the customer that is not being satisfactorily addressed by current solutions. Next, you should present your solution and get feedback on how effective your solution is in the customer's mind. Finally, determine how eager the customer is to try out your solution. If, without prompting from you, the customer requests further meetings or wants to try the product or even offers to pay for it, you have a strong indication that there is potentially a good product/market fit.

- *Customer surveys:* While customer interviews will provide detailed anecdotal information to evaluate your idea, the information may not be statistically valid. You should, therefore, consider conducting detailed surveys using panels provided by panel providers like Lucid or SurveyMonkey. Since the survey recipients are paid to take the surveys, you have to take their responses with a grain of salt. You are looking to mainly validate the results of your interviews and add statistical validity to the responses.

- *Internet ad testing:* Here you would create a landing page that markets your solution and captures an email address for people who are interested in trying the solution. You would then use web and/or mobile advertising to test different messages and drive people to your landing page.

You should start with text advertising to test different messages. Once you honed your message, you could test video ads for your final messaging to determine your success rate at attracting potential customers. The click-through rate and email-capture rate will give you a good sense of how attractive your message is to your potential audience. A click-through rate of 0.5 percent or higher for text ads (with at least three hundred impressions) and 1 percent or higher for video ads (with at least twenty thousand impressions) would be good click-through rates to target. You should also understand the cost per lead (CPL) for the emails that you are capturing. Your CAC (customer acquisition cost) for a paid customer eventually will be much higher but at least you will get a good sense of how expensive it will be to acquire customers once you are ready to launch your offering.

- *Online listening and research:* There are a number of online sources that can provide interesting tidbits of information on customer pain points/frustrations as well as experience with competitive products. These are some of the sources that Madrona Venture Labs surveys to get customer sentiment:

  Reddit

  Quora

  Related books on Amazon with two- or three-star reviews

  Social media posts

  Competitor customer support

  Product hunt-related-product reviews

  GitHub discussion or open Slack communities

  Podcast interviews with competitor management

  Topic-specific blogs

Narrow Customer Focus

Having a clear target market for your product is critical to achieving product/market fit. The narrower the market that you focus on initially, the better. This is contrary to what most startups want to do since they believe that targeting a broader market will maximize customer acquisition, which is essential to raising money. However, a narrow customer focus will ensure that your messaging, marketing efforts, and feature set are highly tuned to your customer needs. The feedback that you get from a narrow customer segment will likely also be remarkably consistent, allowing you to focus your product development efforts. Once you nail product/market fit in a single market, you can then look at expanding into other customer segments or markets.

After determining your initial customer focus, work on developing detailed customer personas and user scenarios. Interview your potential customers to understand their aspirations, critical pain points, and needs. Once you have built these personas, you are in a much stronger position to develop a hypothesis around the pain points that you can address, and identify the features needed in your product to address those pain points.

OfferUp is a top mobile shopping app and competitor to Craigslist that launched initially only in the Seattle market. It leveraged Facebook advertising when it first became available in 2013 to target users in specific zip codes in the Seattle market. In addition, it focused initially on women since they are the primary shoppers who like to put up items for sale and make purchases. The narrow focus on female shoppers in the Seattle market ensured that it could create a critical mass of users in that market transacting in used goods. There was amazing engagement from female shoppers in the Seattle market, which allowed the company to raise the funding needed to expand to additional markets nationwide. As of October 2020,

OfferUp is a top-fifty app in the App Store and has raised $380 million in funding.

Rapid Iteration and Testing

Most of us are now familiar with the concept of first building an MVP (minimum viable product) to test out your value hypotheses as popularized by the lean startup methodology. I am not a big fan of the term "minimum *viable* product." I prefer the term "minimum *delightful* product." With an MVP, you may not get a second shot at customers if they don't find much value in what you have built. It is important to have some core beliefs around critical customer needs and your key feature differentiators that can delight your customers. In the case of the BlackBerry, providing email with end-to-end encryption was critical to establishing early success. Without end-to-end encryption, most corporations wouldn't have authorized the use of BlackBerry for its early adopters. On the other hand, providing a calendar app in order to compete with the Palm

What Is an MVP?

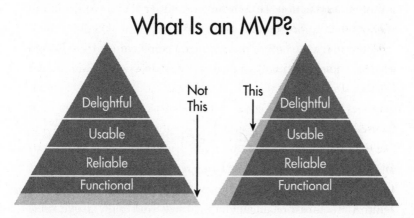

Courtesy of Jussi Pasanen
See Aarron Walter's book *Designing for Emotion*

Copyright © 2017 @danolsen

Figure 1

device was completely orthogonal to its success, and BlackBerry was smart not to build a calendar app initially for its device.

I love the diagram in Figure 1 popularized by Dan Olsen, author of *The Lean Product Playbook* (Dan Olsen adapted this figure from one created by designer Jussi Pasanen, who in turn acknowledges Aarron Walter, Ben Tollady, and Ben Rowe). It shows clearly how to think about building an MVP. Instead of simply doing a partial job of building a bunch of features, build out a specific set of features with a certain level of depth, reliability, usability, and differentiation that delights the customer. As customers react positively to your MVP, you can add more depth in terms of features, taking care always to ensure reliability and usability of the features.

My typical rule of thumb is that for B2C (business to consumer) startups, you shouldn't invest more than three months of product development to get your MVP out. B2B (business to business) offerings take longer, but even then, you shouldn't invest more than six months of product development effort behind an MVP. Start by launching your product on a single platform and iterate your offering to achieve the engagement you desire. For example, if you are a mobile application, launch only on either iOS or Android initially. OfferUp, for example, launched first on the iOS platform. It took another year before the company launched on the Android platform. Eventually, it became available on the web as well.

Focus on Engagement and Retention

During your product iteration process, it is critical that your focus for product development is on driving higher engagement and retention. To measure engagement, track your daily active users (DAU), weekly active users (WAU), and monthly active users (MAU). You should also calculate your DAU/MAU ratio, which is a measure of the frequency of user visits during the month. The DAU/MAU ratio is a function of the category of your app; however, usually apps higher than 20 percent are considered to be good, and 50 percent or higher is world class (Facebook falls into this category). You should also measure critical user activities that are representative of active engagement—for example, how many people are creating or contributing content as opposed to simply consuming content.

To me, retention is an even more important metric than engagement. With high retention, you will have more users using your product for a longer period, which will drive strong word of mouth and user growth. To measure retention, track daily cohorts of users and see how many are returning on Day 1, Day 7, and Day 30. Ideally, you want to see a chart that shows the following daily retention at a minimum:

- Day 1: 40 percent returning
- Day 7: 20 percent returning
- Day 30: 10 percent returning

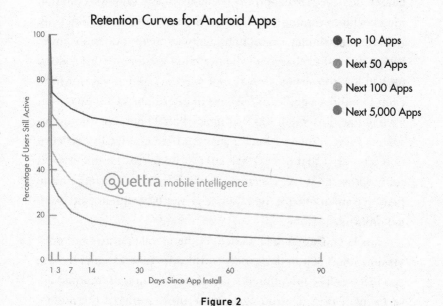

Figure 2

This is the level of retention that you need to have to make it to the list of top 5,000 App store apps (see Figure 2). To drive retention, the core value proposition has to be such that it compels the user to visit frequently. However, you can improve retention by using app notifications or emails with very targeted content—for example, the item in your shopping cart has dropped in price. For enterprise apps, consider integrating with apps like Slack, which you can use to alert the user to new content in your application.

Product Business Model Fit

Once you have achieved product/market fit, the next step is to see if you can achieve product business model fit. In most situations, if you have achieved strong product/market fit, there's a good chance that you will also develop a successful business model for your product. However, this is not always the case. With Livemocha, we achieved strong product/market fit and grew to 15 million members in two hundred different countries with a free offering. However, our timing was off in trying to monetize our application. When we tried to charge for the premium version of our product, we had low conversion (less than 1 percent), which was not sufficient to build a significant business of interest to VCs. The reason we had low conversion was that more than 90 percent of our customers were in international markets where credit card penetration was low at that time (2009–2011). Ultimately, Livemocha was sold to Rosetta Stone, which was looking to build a strong online presence and monetize the Livemocha user base with its paid product offering.

Years later, Duolingo launched on the mobile devices and grew to more than 300 million users worldwide. Like Livemocha, the product was free but offered a premium version that removed advertising. This time around, because they leveraged the mobile payment systems offered on the iOS and Android app stores, they got to a 3 percent conversion rate. With a high installed base, the 3 percent conversion rate has translated to more than $200 million in annual revenues. At the time of this writing, Duolingo is looking to do an IPO on the strength of its significant revenue stream.

PIVOTING
YOUR STARTUP

Getting to product/market fit for your idea can often be a tricky process. Market signals can often by hazy and it is not always clear if your idea is achieving sufficient traction in the marketplace. Founders can also be a stubborn bunch who are often in love with their idea. It is not always easy for a founder or founding team to admit defeat and pivot to a different idea. This is when it is important to have a frank conversation with your board to determine if it is time to pivot. The board often will have the objectivity to dispassionately look at your progress and advise you on whether you should pivot and how you can conserve your cash to successfully execute on a new idea.

The TeamOn Pivot

In early 2000, I launched TeamOn as a SaaS application providing group email and calendaring services for small businesses. My goal was to achieve the same kind of success in the small-business market that Hotmail had achieved in the consumer space. We had good success in acquiring customers through email marketing, reaching several hundred thousand subscribers. Unfortunately, we discovered that usage and retention were not satisfactory, and conversion to a paid version of our software was poor. It turned out that small-business users were still wedded to their ISP email solution and that using a web solution was not attractive because many of the users didn't have a broadband connection at that time. It also required small-business users to change their email address to the address we provided, making the switch even more challenging.

To overcome the challenge of converting users from their existing email solution, we decided to allow users to import their existing email account into TeamOn. Our engineering team did an amazing job of reverse engineering a number of proprietary email systems and added support for POP3/IMAP4 email, AOL Mail, Hotmail, CompuServe, Microsoft Exchange, and Lotus Notes (these were the popular email systems in the early 2000 time frame). Unfortunately, even adding support for these email systems did not materially change the usage of our solution. We had to face the moment of truth that we had not achieved product/market fit with TeamOn.

Fortunately, we had raised more than $15 million in funding in the heyday of the dot-com boom. Unlike many other startups that hired aggressively at that time and then flamed out quickly, I was relatively conservative in my spending, and I still had a good chunk of my investor funding in the bank. We decided that it was time to pivot from our original idea. We also sadly had to cut our staff and let go of more than half our team. It was the most difficult decision that I had made, but I knew that I had to take that step in order to have the opportunity to pivot the company toward a different idea.

After considering several ideas, we ultimately decided to pivot the company in a mobile direction. BlackBerry at that time was gaining notoriety as a great solution for accessing email while on the go. Wireless carriers also started offering phones with built-in data capabilities using GPRS (general packet radio service, a mobile data standard on the 2G and 3G cellular communication networks). While GPRS was very slow (56 kbps), it was still an important innovation that enabled internet access from a mobile device.

Given the success of BlackBerry, we felt that there would be a broad market for consumer mobile users to access their email from their mobile phone. Fortunately for us, we had developed the capability for users to access a range of email systems with TeamOn. We decided to pivot the company to enable mobile phone users to access email from their mobile phone. We would be the only company in the market that provided the capability to access a number of proprietary email systems, not just standard POP3/IMAP4-based email.

Given our unique ability to access various proprietary email systems, we got the attention of a major wireless carrier, T-Mobile, to partner with us to offer our solution to its mobile phone users. At the same time, we approached Research In Motion (the makers of BlackBerry) to see if it would be interested in partnering with us to attract consumer users to its device (at that time, BlackBerry was primarily a corporate email solution). After some initial discussions, RIM made the decision that the capabilities were too strategic and that it would be better off acquiring our company as opposed to partnering with us. We also felt that RIM would be a great acquirer for TeamOn as it had many carrier relationships and would be instrumental in getting the TeamOn solution to leading wireless carriers all over the world.

RIM acquired TeamOn in the summer of 2002. While it took some time to integrate the TeamOn technology into BlackBerry, it ultimately became available to consumers as BlackBerry Internet Service email. This capability was critical to BlackBerry's entry into the consumer market with devices such as the BlackBerry Pearl. Eventually, BlackBerry Internet Service email grew to a significant size, surpassing more than 50 million BlackBerry users.

When to Pivot

Most of the time, it will be obvious when your idea is failing to achieve product/market fit. You will be struggling to acquire customers, user retention will be poor, and you will see low conversion to paid (for freemium offerings). However, you should try everything possible to see if you can make your original idea work before you give up on it. You should especially seek out users who fail to purchase the product or stop using it to really understand what's lacking in your value proposition. Conduct usability studies to see where people are getting stuck with your product so you can remove the roadblocks that are getting in people's way. Study your users systematically by customer segment to see if there are specific segments that are reacting more favorably to your product. Explore changing your business model as well to see if that improves the uptake. For example, if you offer a free trial, consider a freemium strategy where you offer a free version with limited capabilities.

As a general rule of thumb, you should give yourself a good three to six months before deciding whether to pivot to a different idea. You should spend time really understanding if there are aspects of your product that users liked, and pivot around it. For example, Instagram started as a social check-in app called Burbn. The founders discovered that its users didn't really care much about telling their friends where they were. However, they constantly shared photos about the places that they visited.

"We actually got an entire version of Burbn done as an iPhone app, but it felt cluttered and overrun with features. It was really difficult to decide to start from scratch, but we went out on a limb and basically cut everything in the Burbn app except for its photo, comment, and like capabilities. What remained was Instagram," Kevin Systrom said.[1]

Soon thereafter, as a new photo-sharing service, Instagram exploded in terms of usage. A week after its launch, it had a hundred thousand users. A week later, two hundred thousand. A week after that, three hundred thousand. And then it became Apple's App of the Week in the App Store. The rest is history.

Dalton Caldwell from Y Combinator has an interesting framework for evaluating your pivot ideas. You need to evaluate the following criteria:

- How big of an idea is it: 1–10
- Founder/market fit: 1–10
- How easy is it to get started on the idea: 1–10
- Early market feedback from customers: 1–10
- Overall score: 1–10

It is important to keep your investors informed once you decide to pivot. Many founders hate to do this because it means admitting defeat and you feel like a failure. They are also afraid that investors will want to shut down the company and ask for their remaining money back. However, you will find that investors are quite understanding most of the time. They understand that there is a high risk of failure with startups, and that it can often take multiple pivots to get to product/market fit. If you have a strong reputation as a founder and have a promising idea for a pivot, you will find that investors will often put in more money in the company so that you have time to work through your new value proposition.

ARE YOU CUT OUT TO BE AN ENTREPRENEUR?

E ven if you have a great idea, it is worth considering whether
you have the wherewithal to be a successful entrepreneur.
Many people make the mistake of assuming that only
charismatic leaders have the capacity to be great founders. Or they
assume that if you haven't engaged in some entrepreneurial activity
in your youth that you are not cut out to be an entrepreneur. While
these are useful attributes to have, it turns out that there are many
more important factors at play.

. . .

Capacity to Take Financial Risks

Starting a new venture will require you to take substantial financial risk that you need to fully consider before taking the plunge. You will likely be without a salary for a good twelve to eighteen months. Even after you get some funding, you may still have to take a 50 percent pay cut until you raise Series A funding, which could be another twelve months away. Let's say that you are a mid-level manager at a tech company making $250,000 in annual compensation. You are looking at a potential loss of income of $250,000 for the first year and another $125,000 in the second year for a total loss of $375,000 in income. In addition, it is quite likely that you may have to invest another $50,000 to fund the initial development of your product.

If you are relatively fresh out of school, the risk that you are taking will be less significant. You could move back in with your parents and cut your monthly living expenses significantly. However, if you have a family and own a home, you will need to substantially dip into your savings to cover your monthly living expenses or rely on your spouse's income to help make ends meet.

Deep Customer Empathy and Product Orientation

As we have discussed, achieving product/market fit is critical to the success of any startup. You need to have strong customer empathy and a deep understanding of the problems they face so that you can build the right solution for them. As a CEO, even after you have raised funding and hired an experienced management team, you will need to spend a good 30 percent of your time interacting with customers, which you should enjoy doing. You should be constantly updating your understanding of customer usage scenarios and pain points so that you can effectively guide your company in evolving your product.

As the leader of your startup, you need to be knee-deep in defining your product strategy and features. You don't need to be a technical person to effectively guide the product vision. You need to be ready to roll up your sleeves to define the feature set and even go as far as designing the initial UI (user interface) for the product. This is something that I did for all my startups. Certainly, I hired a designer to help me with UI design; however, the initial UX (user experience) framework was designed by me. Even later, when I hired a head of product, I would closely monitor the product evolution to make sure the product stayed true to my vision and was easy to use.

Salesmanship

As an entrepreneur, you need to be selling all the time to be successful. You need to sell potential cofounders, you need to sell customers to try your product, you need to sell investors to fund your company, and you need to sell employees to leave their high-paying jobs and take a pay cut to join your company. As a result, you need to love the idea of selling your vision to all kinds of people, and you have to be good at it. To be clear, you don't need to be a salesperson to do this successfully or have prior sales experience. You need to have a deep understanding of your market, a clear vision for your company, and you need to have strong communication skills to convince people of your point of view.

Perseverance and Mental Fortitude

Entrepreneurs need to have tremendous perseverance and mental fortitude to be successful. You will encounter all sorts of obstacles and challenges along the way that you must overcome. Initially, your challenge will be getting customers and proving product/market fit. Next, you will have to raise funding, which is a never-ending task. Some of your employees may not be a good fit, and you may have to fire them. As I had mentioned earlier, I faced two deep recessions after raising initial funding for my startup. I had to lay off more than 50 percent of my team in my first company. In my second company, I was two months from running out of money before I secured my next round of funding. The stresses of running a startup never end. You have to really believe in your vision and love what you are doing. You have to work hard on maintaining an even keel and convey a sense of calm and confidence to the rest of your team so that they don't lose focus because of the challenges that you are currently facing. The entrepreneurial journey is a marathon, not a 100-meter dash. You need to be good at preserving your energy and keeping your spirits up, so that you have a good chance of making it to the end with a successful outcome.

PART II

COMPANY FORMATION

COMPANY INCORPORATION

Now that you have identified your idea, it is time to think about how to transition from your existing employer (if you are still working your "day job") and form your new company. If you are moonlighting while you are working on your idea, you should be very careful where and how you work on your new startup. Check all your employment-related agreements to ensure that your employer does not have intellectual property (IP) rights to independent work that you have developed or will develop for your startup. To protect your IP as much as possible, you should work on your new company on your own time, using your own personal computer (and other devices including your mobile phone), and at a different location than your current work location. Make sure that you understand the employment and IP laws of the state in which you live, as the relevant laws vary from state to state.

If you are serious about building a substantial business and raising outside capital, you should, as soon as possible, consult with a business attorney who has meaningful experience working with startups. Don't use your uncle who is a divorce lawyer or your sister who is a real estate lawyer. There are a surprising number of pitfalls in setting up a new business, and it becomes more difficult (and more expensive) to fix mistakes as time passes.

Form Your Company

For most startups, it is important that you form a legal entity as soon as possible. Operating your business through a legal entity helps to avoid personal legal responsibility for business debts, obligations, and liabilities. Without forming a legal entity, your default status is that of sole proprietorship (when you own and operate a business by yourself) or a general partnership (when you own and operate your business with one or more individuals). In either case, you would have unlimited personal liability for the obligations of the business.

In addition, setting up the entity properly and as soon as possible helps avoid future disputes over IP and equity ownership. It is not unusual for individuals who are involved in the early ideation phase of a business to drop out or be pushed out of the business. If you haven't set up a legal entity, transferred the relevant IP to the entity, and issued the founders stock (all described in more detail below), you face a significant risk of future disputes as well as the possibility that a potential investor may be scared off from making an investment.

The first step to formation is deciding what type of entity is best. There are many options for legal entities; however, the two most widely used for tech startups are corporations and, to a lesser extent, limited liability companies (LLCs). Corporations can either be taxed as S corporations or C corporations. If you wish to raise financing from venture capital firms, the best option for you will likely be to form a C corp because of tax and other regulatory complications that, in most cases, prevent VCs from investing in S corps or LLCs.

S Corporation

An S corporation is a "Subchapter S Corporation" that has a special tax designation granted by the IRS. S corporations generally are not subject to an entity-level corporate income tax. Instead, the profits and losses are passed through proportionally based on ownership to individual shareholders to report on their personal tax returns. An S corp is often referred to as a "pass-through" or "flow-through" entity because there is only a single level of tax at the owner level. A C corp, on the other hand, is subject to corporate income tax, and if the C corp wants to pay out profits to its owners, the owners are also taxed on the distribution that they receive, resulting in double taxation. Note that you have two months and fifteen days from incorporation to send a notice (Form 2553) to the IRS electing your company to be taxed as an S corp. Without this "S election," the company will default to a C corp for tax purposes.

With an S corp, you can have only up to a hundred shareholders, and all the shareholders have to be US citizens or residents. All shareholders have to be individuals—no legal entities can own stock. You are also only allowed to have one class of stock, which can make it difficult to take outside investment in the form of equity, as investors will typically demand preferred shares with a different set of rights than common shares.

The main benefit of electing an S corp status for your company is that you can pass through your losses to your personal tax return and reduce your overall tax burden, and if the business becomes profitable you can avoid double taxation. However, the losses that you can pass through can, at most, equal your personal investment in the company. For example, if you have $100,000 in losses in the first year and your investment in the company is $25,000 for a 50 percent share of the company, you are eligible to deduct your share of the losses (50 percent of $100,000) but only up to your $25,000 investment. It is, therefore, worthwhile electing an S corp status for your company only if you have made a significant investment in the company.

You can initially make an S corp election and still accept investments from angel investors by taking the investment in the form of a convertible note. The investment, therefore, is in the form of a debt instrument even though it is convertible to preferred shares in the future. At the point at which you raise a Series A round and issue preferred shares, you must convert your company to a C corp. If the financing violates any of the S corp restrictions described above (which it almost certainly would), your S corp will automatically become a C corp.

One final note: If you start off as an S corp, your shares will not meet the requirements for qualified small business stock (QSBS), which can provide substantial future tax benefits as described below. If you are successful with your startup, your share price will increase significantly in value, creating a substantial gain when you sell the company. The first $10 million in gains from selling qualified small business stock (QSBS) can be eligible for up to 100 percent exclusion from federal income tax.

LLC (Limited Liability Company)

An LLC is a business structure that combines the "pass-through" tax benefits of an S corp or a sole proprietorship with the legal benefits of limited personal liability. Like an S corp, it is possible to pass on your losses to your personal tax return and reduce your tax burden. Although an LLC with two or more members is generally treated as a "pass-through" entity, it can also choose to be taxed as a C corp.

An LLC is typically more complicated and expensive to form compared to a corporation. The internal operations of an LLC are covered by a mutually agreed upon "operating agreement" as opposed to the "articles of incorporation," "bylaws," and "shareholder agreement" for an S corp or a C corp. Unlike an S corp, it is possible to create multiple classes of ownership interests in an LLC to account for different preferences and rights, there are no citizenship or residency requirements, legal entities can be owners, and you can have an unlimited number of owners. However, it is not possible to issue incentive stock options (ISOs) to employees, which is a standard practice for most startups. ISOs have significant potential tax advantages compared to non-qualified stock options (NSOs), as described later in this section.

Given the expense and the disadvantages, I don't recommend that startups organize their company as an LLC. It is much better to consider an S corp for initial incorporation, but only if you are looking to benefit from the losses in the initial years. Otherwise, it is far more preferable to incorporate as a C corp from the start, because it is much more investor friendly, and you can also benefit from treating your shares as QSBS stock.

C Corporation

A C corp is typically the best option for founders to consider in incorporating their company. There are no restrictions in the number or types of shareholders. You can have multiple classes of stock—in addition to common shares, you can have "preferred" shares that you can offer to investors with better preferences and rights. C corp shares can also be designated as QSBS stock, which offers significant tax benefits to the founders when they sell their shares. You can offer incentive stock options to employees, which have significant tax benefits to them. Note that you can only offer NSOs to contractors, but more on this later.

Like an S corp, a C corp is governed by a board of directors. The board must designate officers of the company to manage the day-to-day operations of the company. The board may also delegate certain decisions to committees such as a compensation committee that determines the compensation for the officers of the company or an audit committee that provides oversight over the company's financial functions.

A C corp can raise capital in the form of equity or debt. If the company is private, care must be taken to make sure that the company is raising capital only from accredited investors. Technically, you can raise money from unaccredited investors, but it is typically not worth jumping through the hoops to do this. Generally, an individual is an accredited investor if he or she meets the following:

- Any natural person whose individual net worth, or joint net worth with that person's spouse, exceeds $1 million (excluding the net value of their primary residence).
- Any natural person who had an individual income in excess of $200,000 in each of the two most recent years or joint income with that person's spouse in excess of $300,000 in each of those years and has a reasonable expectation of reaching the same income level in the current year.

One important point to note is that *all* securities offers and sales are subject to the general anti-fraud provisions of the Securities Act of 1933 and Securities Exchange Act of 1934, which means that all documents or other information provided to prospective investors must be accurate and not misleading. They may not omit any information that would render them misleading in any material respect.

Qualified Small Business Stock (QSBS)

As mentioned earlier, if you own qualified small business stock, you can eliminate all or a significant portion of your capital gain. With QSBS, you can avoid paying federal tax on gains of up to $10 million or ten times your tax basis (basis for this purpose is equal to the amount of cash plus the fair market value of any property contributed to the corporation in exchange for the stock).

Here are some basic requirements for your stock to qualify as QSBS:

- Company is a domestic C corporation engaged in certain types of businesses (which would include most technology startups).
- Stock is issued after August 10, 1993.
- Stock is acquired by taxpayer directly from the company for money, property (other than stock), or services (limited exceptions to this rule).
- The tax basis of the total gross assets of the corporation at all times from August 10, 1993, until immediately after the issuance of the taxpayer's stock must be less than $50 million.

In order to benefit from the tax exclusion, you have to have held the stock for at least five years. However, it is possible to do tax-free rollovers into another QSBS stock and combine the holding periods.

How and Where to Incorporate

To form a corporation, the incorporator files Articles or a Certificate of Incorporation (the name depends on the jurisdiction) in the state where you want to incorporate, along with a filing fee. While it might seem natural for startups to incorporate in the state of their domicile, I highly recommend that you incorporate your company in Delaware. In fact, most VCs will require you to incorporate in Delaware if you haven't already done so. Delaware is considered to be a very business friendly state. It has a well-developed and well-understood body of law. It has business friendly statutes and has a special separate court system that handles only business disputes.

It is, however, somewhat more expensive to incorporate and operate your company in Delaware. You have to work through registered agents and incur filing fees. The initial incorporation fees are slightly higher than in most other states. In addition, on an annual basis, you need to pay franchise taxes to the state. You have to pay these fees in addition to registering in the state of your domicile, for which you will pay additional fees. Delaware will send annual tax notices stating the default amount of tax based on the number of authorized shares, but there is an alternative calculation of the franchise tax based on assets that will lower the tax bill for most startups by 90–95 percent. I still remember the "heart attack" I got when I first got my bill, but fortunately, I was able to substantially lower my tax bill because of the assets we had.

HOW TO SPLIT FOUNDER EQUITY

Now that you formed your company, one of the key decisions that you have to make is how to split up the equity in the company among founders. Oftentimes, to avoid conflict, founders decide to split up equally. However, that can be the wrong decision especially if some of the founders are bringing significantly different contributions to the table. In addition, a 50/50 split can result in a deadlock on important decisions, most of which will require a majority vote.

Deciding how to split up founder equity can certainly be an awkward process especially when there are multiple cofounders with different experiences and contributions. Several years ago, I came across a situation where five cofounders worked on a startup idea for more than six months and then split up because they couldn't agree on how to divide the equity among themselves. Clearly you want to avoid this situation and I recommend that you discuss equity splits even before you start working on your idea with your cofounder(s).

Cash Investment

If you and/or your cofounder(s) are planning on investing actual cash into the company, it should be treated like any other outside investment. Let's say that you and your cofounder are both investing $50,000 in the business. You can then select an appropriate valuation for the company and calculate the equity that each of you would get as a result. To determine an appropriate valuation for the company, you can consult with local angel investors to get their feedback on the company's valuation given the team composition and the progress you have made.

Let's say that you valued the company at $1 million. Since you each invested $50,000 in the business, the post-money valuation of the company would be $1,100,000. Each of you would then get $50,000/$1,100,000, or 4.5 percent, of the company's equity. The remaining equity can be divided based on the rules outlined below.

Employee Option Pool

I recommend that you set aside between 15 and 20 percent of the company's equity for an employee option pool from which you would grant options to employees you hire. Assuming you set aside 20 percent for the option pool and both cofounders invest $50,000 each into the business, that would leave 71 percent of the company's equity to be split between you and your cofounder.

Utilizing an Experienced Arbiter

You will find many articles on the internet with detailed guidance on how to split founder equity based on a variety of factors (time investment, expertise, startup role, and so on). However, even with those parameters, you could still end up in a difficult negotiation with your cofounder(s) on how to split up the founder equity. I, therefore, recommend that you find an experienced and well-respected founder or investor to come up with the equity split recommendation that you all have to abide by. That person can interview each of the cofounders to understand their contributions and then recommend the equity split that you should follow. This will result in significantly less contention and bad feelings among the founders. Assuming that you can't find a mutually agreeable arbiter, I have outlined some additional guidelines that you can utilize to decide on the equity splits.

Time Investment

I highly recommend that you and your cofounder(s) work full-time on your idea (even if you are moonlighting). Anything less than a full-time commitment will not get you very far in making progress with your startup. If someone can't make a full-time commitment, then he or she should be treated like a part-time employee and receive equity from the option pool that you have set aside for employees.

Idea Development

Ideas can be a dime a dozen as a startup's success will depend largely on execution. However, if you have spent a few months seriously validating the idea before recruiting a cofounder, then you should get some credit for developing the idea. Or perhaps you are a technical founder and you have already developed a prototype for your idea. Idea validation should get you a 5 to 10 percent premium, whereas IP development should get you a 20 to 25 percent premium, depending on how much time you have invested in developing the IP.

CEO Role

If there are two cofounders, you can't split the equity 50/50 as you could end up in a tie in deciding contentious issues. Since the CEO has to be the final arbiter of decisions, he or she should receive more equity. Investors also value the CEO role compared to other roles in the company and will grant more equity to a CEO if they are hiring an external CEO. The CEO should get a 5 percent premium for taking on that role.

Successful Entrepreneurs

If one of the founders has been a successful entrepreneur before, that person can considerably increase the chances of success in raising funding, getting a higher valuation, and improving the prospects for the company. He or she may command anywhere from a 50 to a 100 percent premium for bringing prior startup success and expertise to the company.

Doing the Math

Imagine you have a technical founder who has developed a working prototype for the product. The technical founder then convinces a successful startup CEO to join the company as a CEO and co-founder. Both start with a 50/50 split in terms of shares. The technical founder gets another five shares for idea validation and twenty-five shares for IP development. The CEO cofounder gets five more shares for being a CEO and fifty more shares for being a successful entrepreneur. As a result, you end up with eighty shares for the technical cofounder and 105 shares for the CEO, leading to a 43 percent to 57 percent split in terms of equity. While it may seem unfair to give the CEO a greater share, it might be worthwhile if that person is able to help the technical founder raise funding at a high valuation, leading to less dilution and higher equity stake post-funding.

Vesting

Once you have decided on how to split founder equity, it is important that each founder agrees to a vesting schedule for the equity allocated to them. Typically, the vesting takes place on a monthly schedule over a four-year period, although I have done it for less (three years). Note that there should be no vesting for any cash investment that any cofounder makes into the company.

Splitting equity is one of the first important decisions that you will make with your cofounder(s). It will give you a good sense for how much you respect your cofounders and what type of relationship you will have over the long term. It is important that you be fair in your discussions because you want your cofounders to feel that they have an important stake in the business. Seek advice from respected entrepreneurs/investors in the community so you all get through the discussion with the feeling that you were all treated fairly.

83(b) Election

One of the most important tax decisions that a founder can make is whether to file an 83(b) election under the federal tax code for stock awards that are subject to vesting. The default under the federal tax code is that you owe taxes each time a portion of your stock vests on the spread between the price that you paid for that portion of the stock and the fair market value of that stock on the date of vesting. If your company is successful, the fair market value of your stock will increase and the taxes that you owe will be substantial even though you may not have the ability to sell your stock. You can avoid this problem by filing an 83(b) election, where you pay taxes on the spread between the price you paid for all the stock and the fair market value on the date of issuance of that stock. Normally, that spread would be zero, so you would owe no taxes when you file the 83(b) election, and you would owe no taxes as the stock vests. **You must file the election with the Internal Revenue Service within thirty days of your stock grant or purchase and there is no remedy for a delayed filing.**

A Section 83(b) election is made by sending a letter to the IRS requesting to be taxed on the date the restricted stock was granted or purchased rather than on the scheduled vesting dates. If the restricted stock is purchased for an amount equal to its fair market value, an 83(b) election will result in no recognition of income as of the purchase date. However, when you later sell your stock, if it has been more than one year from the date of grant, the additional gain will be taxed at the long-term capital gains rate.

FUNDAMENTALS OF CAP TABLES

A cap (capitalization) table, at the most fundamental level, is a ledger of all the equity that is owned by various entities (founders, employees, consultants, investors, and so on) in the company. It is very important that you keep an accurate record of the equity ownership by various entities at all times. Most investors will ask for a cap table when you seek funding, and it will determine the per share price that will be used in the financing.

Note that in calculating your ownership in the company, you should do so on a "fully diluted basis"—in other words, taking into account all your option grants, your remaining option pool, and any warrants that you have issued. The share price for any financing will also be calculated by dividing the pre-money valuation (more on the definition of "pre-money" in the next section) by the fully diluted number of shares.

An Entrepreneur's Journey

To understand how cap tables work, let's follow the funding journey of a hypothetical company, ABC, Inc., started by John and Jane Doe through Series A funding. John and Jane decide to split their stake 50/50. In addition, they set aside an option pool of 20 percent for their employees. They also decide to set up the company with a total of 10 million authorized shares with a par value of $0.001 per share, which is pretty typical. The cap table will now look as follows:

Capitalization Table for ABC, Inc.

Shareholder	Shares	Price	Ownership
John Doe	4,000,000	$0.001	40 percent
Jane Doe	4,000,000	$0.001	40 percent
Employee Option Pool	2,000,000	$0.001	20 percent
Total	10,000,000		

Seed Round

Now let's say the company raises a seed round of $500,000 from a seed VC firm, Vista Capital, as a convertible note with a valuation cap of $4 million and a 20 percent discount to the next round. This means that when the company raises a Series A, the valuation that the angel investors will get for their shares will be the lower of $4 million or 80 percent of the valuation paid by the Series A investors. Since no new shares were issued at this stage, the cap table remains the same.

Series A Funding

Now imagine that the company is doing well and has reached a milestone of $1 million ARR (annual recurring revenues). This is typically the milestone at which most mainstream VCs will consider funding a company. The company gets a term sheet (a nonbinding agreement that spells out the terms and conditions of an investment) from Sunrise Venture Capital to fund the company with $6 million in funding at a pre-money valuation of $24 million. The term sheet also stipulates an employee option pool of 20 percent post-funding.

Since the term sheet requires an employee option pool of 20 percent post-funding, the employee option pool will need to be increased by another 1 million shares (this requires an iterative calculation that's a bit complex to describe here). This results in a total number of shares of 11 million prior to funding. The share price for the seed investor will be calculated as $4 million/11 million shares = $0.36, since they have a $4 million valuation cap, which is lower than 80 percent of $24 million. On the other hand, the share price for the Series A investor will be calculated as $24 million/11 million shares = $2.18. The resulting cap table looks as follows:

Capitalization Table for ABC, Inc.

Shareholder	Shares	Price	Ownership
John Doe	4,000,000	$0.001	26 percent
Jane Doe	4,000,000	$0.001	26 percent

Employee Option Pool	3,017,026	$0.001	20 percent
Vista Capital	1,377,128	$0.363	9 percent
Sunrise Venture Capital	2,754,256	$2.178	18 percent
Total	**15,148,410**		

Note that the common shares owned by John and Jane Doe and the employee option pool are still listed at $0.001, which is not quite correct. Post-funding, the company will need to do a 409A valuation (more on this in the next chapter) to determine a new valuation of the common shares. The common shares will have a value that will be significantly less than that of the preferred shares issued to investors, since they have many preferences and rights that the common shareholders don't have. For example, they have a liquidation preference—they get their money first in the event of a sale, and if the sale price is not high enough, there may be no distribution to common shareholders.

There are many tools available like Carta and Capshare to manage your equity. However, in the initial stages, it will be sufficient to manage your cap table using a simple spreadsheet.

STARTUP OPTIONS

S tartup options are among the most common and important forms of compensation for startups. An option is a contract that allows the grantee to purchase shares of a company at a fixed price (exercise price) in the future. Typically, grantees are given the right to exercise their options over a ten-year period while they are employed with the company or within three months of ending their employment/advisory relationship with the company. There's also a vesting period that details how many options one can exercise during the term of the option.

While most people are familiar with options at a high level, there are many aspects of options that you should understand as a founder before you start granting options to employees, advisors, and board members.

ISOs Versus NSOs

There are two types of options—incentive stock options (ISOs) and non-qualified stock options (NSOs). ISOs can be granted only to employees. NSOs should be granted to advisors and board members, though some startups grant NSOs to employees as well—for example, Microsoft granted NSOs to employees in its early days.

ISOs generally afford better tax treatment compared to NSOs. You should consult your accountant to understand the tax implications, as they can be quite complicated.

Vesting for employee stock options typically takes place over four years with 25 percent vesting after one year and monthly vesting thereafter. Vesting for advisors is typically monthly for the period for which you have hired the advisor. The Founder Institute offers guidelines[1] for how much equity to offer advisors.

409A Valuation of Shares

Before granting options, you need to get approval for the option grant from your company's board, which should be recorded in the board minutes. To avoid IRS penalties, the exercise price for the grant should be set at or above the FMV (fair market value) of the company's common shares on that date. However, the FMV of the common shares cannot be an arbitrary number that you or your board determine. Section 409A of the IRS code requires that the company conduct an independent valuation of its share price. Typically, this is done by hiring a reputable third-party valuation firm, which can cost between $5,000 and $15,000. You want to select a firm that has a good relationship with one of the four national accounting firms or a large regional firm. The reason is that these firms will one day audit your 409A valuation, and you don't want a situation where they invalidate the valuations that were done. These days, companies like Carta and Capshare can do the 409A valuation at a cheaper price than their competition. However, you should check to see whether their valuations have been accepted as valid by the large accounting firms.

Be careful about "pressuring" your valuation provider to artificially lower the share price for your options. If the company is successful, the difference in the option price will not be material. However, if you get challenged by the IRS, the penalty for not accurately pricing your options can be significant for your employees. The IRS can also levy up to a 20 percent penalty on stock options that vested prior to that tax year. In addition, the employees will have to pay ordinary income tax for the difference between the FMV of the shares and the option exercise price for all the options they have vested and every time they vest new shares.

You should ideally have a 409A valuation done right after a financing event since your share price will have changed at that point. The 409A valuation should be done before any new options are granted to establish a safe harbor. The 409A valuations are valid for a maximum of twelve months after the valuation date or until a material event. A material event is an occurrence that could reasonably be expected to affect a company's stock price. For most early-stage startups, a qualified financing is the most common type of material event.

Establishing an Option Pool

Most investors will require you to establish an option pool that is between 15 and 20 percent of your fully diluted number of shares when raising a seed or Series A financing round so you can grant options to employees and advisors without further dilution to the investors. It is important that you create an option pool budget for the options that you plan to grant until the next financing that is approved by the board. This will ensure that you have enough options to cover your hiring plans during that period. You should also record all your option grants in a spreadsheet or utilize a tool like Carta.

Options are a valuable form of incentive you can offer to employees to invest their heart and soul into the company. Typically, the first stock grant is the biggest option that employees receive upon joining a company. However, make sure to periodically make additional smaller grants to keep your employees motivated and to ensure that they remain with the company for a long time.

PART III

FUNDRAISING

OVER THE COURSE OF THREE different startups, I have been fortunate to have raised more than $30 million in funding from both angels and VC firms. Twice, I have raised funding when investors were investing freely, but even then, raising funding was never an easy process. Once, I raised $8 million in funding during the depths of the global financial crisis. It was a down round (when a company needs more funding and must offer shares at a lower price because its valuation is lower than during the previous round of financing), as funding was very hard to come by and, as a result, we had to suffer substantial dilution. Fundraising can be a long and arduous process that can take anywhere from three to six months to complete if you have an attractive value proposition for investors. However, it is one of the most important tasks that a startup CEO needs to undertake to make sure their company has enough funding to get to the next milestone.

Besides raising money, the fundraising process will also help crystallize your business plan and messaging. Even if you are not able to raise funding from a specific investor, you should leverage the process to get feedback from every investor with whom you meet. This will help you further refine your pitch, which will allow you to be a lot more successful both in recruiting employees and selling to potential customers and partners.

In this section, we will explore different sources of funding and the types of investment vehicles such as convertible notes, SAFEs, Series Seed, and so on. There is a lot of complicated terminology describing how VCs invest their money; however, it is not hard to understand. Most of the terms are fairly standard, but it is important that you understand the implications of each so they don't come back to bite you later. For example, you might think that you have a 40 percent ownership in the company—however, if your investors have a liquidation preference and the company is sold for a low valuation, they may end up with most of the proceeds, and you may not get your 40 percent share.

Before you get into this section, I will warn you that it is pretty dense. I discuss different funding vehicles and the intricacies of a term sheet. If you like, you can skim through this section, but you should definitely read it in detail as you get ready for fundraising for your company.

EARLY-STAGE FUNDING SOURCES

Typically, when most startups are launched, founders will bootstrap by moonlighting while they continue working at their previous company. This can often be a good way to reduce your risk, allowing you to make the jump to working full-time on your startup only after you have raised enough funding. However, progress can be slow, especially if your current job is more than full-time, and you may lack the proper motivation to make progress on your startup if you have the luxury of a comfy job. Your current job may also make it difficult to travel to potential customer locations or to provide proper support for a successful customer experience.

I have seen situations where founders leave their current jobs but start a consulting gig while working on their startup. They use the funds they raise through their consulting work to pay their own salaries and also fund product development. While this can be a legitimate strategy, it carries significant risk to get your startup off to a good start. Unlike a full-time job, consulting work has higher risk in that it leaves little time to make progress on your startup. You also have to be careful to set up two different companies—one for your consulting work and the other for your startup. Investors don't like investing in a single company that mixes two different business models.

Family and Friends

Family and friends are often the first source of funding for startups. They are likely to be supportive, as they know you well and would like to see your venture succeed. You should make sure that the investors understand the risk they are taking, and that they could potentially lose all their money. You should also keep them apprised of the progress of the company, the highlights and lowlights, so they understand that you are giving it your best shot. This will result in less strained relationships and bad feelings if your venture does not succeed.

The investment from friends and family should be structured like any other investment from professional investors. The best course of action would be to structure the investment as a convertible note with a reasonable cap reflecting the current valuation of the company.

Angel Investors

Angel investors can be a varied group of investors. There's no prototypical angel investor. Typically, every major city with a significant tech community has a group of super angel investors who have invested in a large number of deals. Because of their reputation, they will receive a significant amount of deal flow and can afford to be selective about the deals they invest in. They will also typically be the lead investor that will set the terms of the deal that other angel investors will adhere to. These super angels will typically invest between $100,000 to $250,000 in a deal, whereas the average angel investor will invest between $25,000 to $100,000.

Angel investors typically like to invest with other angel investors whom they know. Either they will be in a formal investing group with other angels or they will be part of an informal group of angel investors with whom they will invest. In Seattle, for example, the top angel groups include the Alliance of Angels and the Keiretsu Forum (which has a nationwide presence). Some of these groups, including the Keiretsu Forum, charge a hefty fee to present to their group.

It can often take quite a bit of time to get in front of these angel groups, which you should take into account in planning your timeline for fundraising. Once you present to the angel group, some members will show interest and decide to move forward to conduct further due diligence on the company. However, oftentimes, the due diligence process can be haphazard, with no clear leader to drive the overall process. Once the group decides to move forward on the investment, it typically picks a lead investor to negotiate the terms of the deal.

Incubators

People often confuse the terms "accelerators" and "incubators," thinking they mean the same concept. However, there are important differences between the two types of organizations that founders should understand before they join a specific program. Incubators often come up with their own ideas that they "incubate" and then spin off into new companies. They have a set process for validating their ideas, and often they will reject dozens of concepts before settling on a few that they build out.

Like accelerators, incubators will also accept external founders and ideas. They will help validate these ideas, and once they decide to move forward with the idea, they will provide the initial funding and help with recruiting a management team as well as help raise funding for the company. However, unlike accelerators, incubators will typically demand a significantly higher equity stake in the company for early involvement in the validation phase. Often, an incubator can take as much as 25 percent of equity post-seed funding in the company that they incubate. However, they also invest a significant amount of their money and resources to build out prototypes and to conduct the market research to validate their idea.

Madrona Venture Labs (MVL) is a well-known incubator that was spun out of Madrona Venture Group, a top VC firm based in Seattle. MVL has incubated more than twelve companies, including well-known companies such as Rover, which has achieved unicorn status ("unicorn" refers to startups worth more than $1 billion, a statistical rarity analogous to the mythical creature). MVL started by incubating ideas out of its own labs before spinning them out. They would develop and validate the idea, and once they had done that, they would hire a management team and help raise funding for the idea. However, they eventually discarded this approach when they found that hired management teams didn't truly understand the contributions they had made. They also questioned the stake that MVL took for bootstrapping the startup.

MVL now takes a different approach for incubating ideas. They look for founders in markets that are of interest to them. Once they find founders with promising ideas, they bring them into MVL as EIRs (Entrepreneurs in Residence) and pay them a stipend. They then engage with the founders on a three-phase plan to incubate their idea. In Phase I, they work with the founder to research the market opportunity and meet with potential customers. They also talk to potential investors to get their feedback on the idea. At the end of Phase I, they make a go-no-go decision based on their research. If they decide to move to Phase II, they form and fund the company to the tune of $250,000 to $300,000. For their investment, they receive a significant stake in the company. They also help the founder recruit a cofounder and other key employees. At this point, they start building an MVP (minimum viable product) and go back to potential customers they had interviewed to see if they would sign up for a pilot. If it makes sense, the team will also build out a landing page and test the concept with online advertising. They also invest more time talking to Madrona Venture Group and securing a commitment for funding from one of the Madrona managing directors. The goal of Phase II is to end up with a well-defined MVP and a solid number of pilot customers. The final phase involves building out an investor pitch and lining up investors for a $3 million round in the company. The company will also try to convert a number of its pilot customers into paying customers.

MVL also runs a Startup Weekend–style incubation program called GoVertical in partnership with TiE Seattle, which brings together more than fifty business professionals, software developers, and data scientists to work on eight to ten promising ideas around specific technologies such as machine learning and blockchain. Two of the companies that graduated from this program have raised Series A funding.

If you are a very early-stage founder with an idea that has not yet been validated, you should consider partnering with an incubator to validate your idea and build out your team. Here are some of the questions you should ask of any incubator program you are evaluating:

- What is your process for validating your idea? How long will it take? What resources will you allocate?
- Will you help in building out working prototypes for our idea?
- How much funding will you provide?
- What are examples of successful ideas that you have incubated?
- Who are some of the investors in the companies that you have incubated?
- How much equity will you take in my company? In what form?

Accelerators

In contrast to incubators, accelerators generally work with startups that are further along in their maturity. They typically like to work with startups that have at least two founders and a product that's ready to be tested with potential customers. Most accelerators have an application process and accept startups in batches for a three- to four-month program. They generally have a strong network of mentors they bring in to advise the startups. Unlike incubators, they offer no help in validating the idea or any resources to build out prototypes. Some will also provide a shared coworking office space where startups can work next to each other. This can be very valuable—it is a great way to meet other founders who can brainstorm with you on challenges that you face. At the end of the program, they host a Demo Day that is attended by well-respected, local investors.

Some of the top accelerators include Y Combinator, Techstars, and 500 Startups. Many universities also offer their own accelerator programs to help student-founded startups.

Many accelerators will provide funding for startups for the duration of their program. For example, Y Combinator invests $125,000 using a "post-money SAFE" that converts to 7 percent ownership stake in the company. Techstars, on the other hand, contributes $20,000 for 6 percent common stock ownership in a company. They will also invest $100,000 in the form of a convertible note.

Accelerators can often be a good path for startups to pursue even if they give up a significant portion of their equity to join the program. Accelerators can offer access to experienced mentors and former graduates who can provide valuable guidance to the company. Most important, through their investor relationships and Demo Day events, they can provide invaluable visibility for startups who may otherwise struggle to get in front of well-known investors.

Here are some of the questions that you should ask of any accelerator program you are evaluating:

- What are the services that you offer to startups in your program?
- Can you provide bios of some of the mentors who will be involved with the program?
- How much funding will you provide? How much equity stake will you take in my company for the funding you provide, and how will it be structured?
- Who are the investors that have attended previous Demo Days? Who are the investors in the last two batches of your program?
- What are some of the successful companies that have graduated from your program?

Venture Capital Seed Funds

While VCs typically participate in Series A funding and beyond, a number of VCs will also get involved in seed funding at an earlier stage—in other words, where a company is raising $1 to $3 million or less in funding. A number of large VC firms have a seed funding program to invest in seed stage companies. They may also opportunistically choose to invest in a few seed stage companies so they can get in early into promising companies. There are also a number of pure VC seed funds—for example, Founders Co-op out of Seattle and Z5 Capital out of the Bay Area—that solely invest in seed funding rounds. I typically recommend that startups avoid getting seed funding from large VC firms and instead stick to raising funding from VC seed funds. If you raise seed funding from a large VC firm, most follow-on funds will want to know if the original VC firm is planning on leading the next round in the company. If they don't plan to do so, it creates a "signaling" risk that there's something wrong with the company (even if the company is doing well on most measures). The other issue is that a large VC firm will simply not devote the resources to help out companies where they have made only a small investment. They will typically also not join the board of directors for the company, which means that you will miss out on valuable feedback that you would otherwise get from an experienced investor. Seed VC firms, on the other hand, will join your board and will devote the time and resources to help the company reach its next milestone. They also typically do not lead follow-up rounds, so there's little signaling risk compared to a large VC firm (they will invest pro rata, however, to maintain their ownership stake in the company).

Entrepreneur Journey

There are many paths that entrepreneurs can take to raise funding for their startup depending on the quality and experience of the founding team. Let's consider a few examples.

Experienced Founder: If you are an experienced prior founder or startup veteran, you probably have the easiest path to fund your company. You have the ability to form an experienced founding team and go to prior investors to raise funding. I invested in a company called Suplari that was formed by founders with significant prior startup experience (as individual contributors). I knew one of the founders and thought highly of him, which resulted in my investment. The company raised a $3.1 million seed round from Madrona Venture Group and local angels on the basis of a PowerPoint presentation because of their prior reputation and the quality of their idea.

In another example, I invested in Ally, a SaaS solution for managing OKRs (objectives and key results) whose CEO was a successful entrepreneur. The CEO had a successful exit with his previous company and chose to bootstrap Ally. To conserve money, he partnered with a cofounder in India to build a development team there. He raised a $3 million seed round following impressive early traction as his first fundraise from local seed funds and prominent local angel investors.

Solo Business Founder: If you are a solo business founder with deep domain expertise and an idea but no technical cofounder, you will have a tough time getting out of the gate. In that situation, you should strongly consider working with an incubator. They will help validate the idea in the market and also help with the initial prototyping and recruitment of a technical cofounder and the development team. They will also help you with fundraising, which can be a significant benefit if you have no prior reputation as a founder. However, as I mentioned, for the work that they do, they will take a significant "sweat equity" in the company.

Brian Camposano is a great example of a solo business founder who had significant finance experience. He was a CFO at Docker, Inc., and had worked at Deutsche Bank and Concur Technologies (now SAP Concur). As a CFO at Docker, he had experienced significant pain in managing the budgeting and forecasting process and felt that a better collaboration and data aggregation tool could be built to address the need. He joined MVL as an EIR (Entrepreneur in Residence) in March 2020 to explore the idea. It didn't take much to convince MVL and they quickly formed and funded a company to pursue the idea. MVL hired an outsourced team to start building the product and helped the company recruit the initial team as well. Five months later, the company raised a $4.9 million seed round from Madrona Venture Group.

Inexperienced Founding Team: If you are not an experienced founding team with both a business and a technical founder, you will likely find it hard to raise any angel funding initially. Your best bet is to bootstrap your company until you have a product developed and ideally some initial traction. At that point, you can consider raising money from angel investors. Another strong option for you to consider is to apply to an accelerator like Y Combinator or Techstars. You will get some initial funding and valuable advice from experienced mentors. Most important, they have the ability to bring well-known investors to their Demo Day and give your company visibility in front of these investors.

Airbnb is a great example of a company that was bootstrapped and funded in this fashion. The founders had mainly design experience but were able to find a technical resource to build the initial website. They were accepted by Y Combinator and received valuable advice from Paul Graham to move to New York City to get traction going for their site. The rest is history. Airbnb is likely to become Y Combinator's best investment to date.

THE FUNDRAISING PROCESS

F undraising for your startup is often a long and arduous process even for founders who have strong reputations and good ideas. The timeline to raise funding can be anywhere from three months at a minimum to more like four to six months if you have a strong team and idea. You need to put in a lot of prep time for your investor pitch, research the investors you want to approach, and network with other founders who can help you to navigate your way to the investors on your list.

If you are raising funding at a pre-seed stage, you will typically be dealing with angel investors who are writing $25,000 to $50,000 checks. As a result, it can take a fairly long time to round up enough investors to fill your round. For example, if you are planning on raising a $500,000 round, you will likely need to meet with twenty angel investors, assuming half of them invest in the company at $50,000 each. Ideally, you want to quickly identify a lead investor who can negotiate the terms of your raise and help introduce you to other angel investors. You can somewhat short-circuit your time and be more efficient by pitching to angel groups. However, it can take two to three months to get on the calendar of an angel group. Thereafter, the due diligence process itself can take another four to six weeks to complete and another two weeks to negotiate the term sheet. *Ideally, when you go in front of an angel group, you should have half your round already filled.* This will create a sense of momentum and scarcity that can drive interest among the investor group.

As you move to the seed stage or Series A funding, you will be dealing primarily with VC firms. Make sure that you have done due diligence on each firm that you plan to approach. You should make sure that they are investing in the markets or categories that your product is targeting and that they have not invested in a competing company. You should also figure out which specific partner at the firm has the closest affinity to the market that you are targeting. Finally, you should figure out who in your network has a strong connection with the partner at each VC firm you wish to approach. You should leverage your pre-seed or angel investors to help you develop the target VC list, and reach out to them.

In seeking an introduction to the VC firm, provide your contact with a short blurb about your company. Make sure it is no longer than two paragraphs and include a short description of your value proposition, traction that you have achieved to date, and background information about the founders. It is generally a good idea to also include a five- to six-slide version of your pitch deck that provides enough information about your startup to pique the interest of the VC firm. Make sure that your contact forwards this information to the contact at the VC firm with an enthusiastic note explaining why the contact is excited about the potential of your company.

You should generally try to time your initial investor pitches to be around the same time and keep the investor discussions going on a similar timeline. The reason this is important is that you want to receive all the investor term sheets at around the same time so you can play them off against one another. Generally, investor term sheets have a short life span, typically one to two days, in which you have to respond, though you can probably get the deadline extended for up to a week. However, it is not always possible to start all investor discussions at the same time. In that case, if a specific investor is ahead of the rest, try to slow down those discussions so that the rest of the investors have an opportunity to catch up.

Generally, the process with a specific VC will involve an initial meeting with the lead partner for the VC firm followed by another meeting or two to go into more detail on specific topics of interest to the lead partner. Often the lead partner will bring an associate and/or another partner from the firm to these meetings. This will be followed by due diligence by the associate and the lead partner, including customer calls, so be prepared to provide the VC firms with team and customer references. The VC firm will also want to do in-depth technical due diligence of your technology stack and architecture. Once the due diligence has been done, the lead partner will then schedule a pitch to all the partners at the VC firm. After that meeting, the VC firm will hold a vote to decide whether to invest in the company and then issue a term sheet.

Typically, at the initial meeting, the VC firm will ask you how much you would like to raise and if you had a specific valuation expectation. I generally recommend that you provide a specific number that you would like to raise as opposed to a range, so you look very deliberate in your capital raise plans. This number should also be reflected in the financials that are part of the investor pitch.

When it comes to discussing your valuation expectations, however, I recommend that you don't provide a specific number. You should tell the investors that you will let the market dictate the terms. In a sense, by discussing the amount that you wish to raise, you are signaling a specific valuation range. For example, if you are looking to raise $6 million in a Series A round, you are signaling an $18 to $24 million pre-money valuation range, as VCs typically expect to own 20 to 25 percent of your company in a Series A scenario.

Sometimes VCs will also ask you who else you are talking to. The answer should always be "the usual suspects." Don't make the mistake of naming specific VC firms because they will immediately contact the other VC firms to compare notes on the investment. If the other VC firms have formed a negative opinion about your company, it will create unnecessary hurdles for you.

Generally, for the investor meetings, I recommend that at least two cofounders attend. Investors like to see both cofounders in action and, in particular, how they interact. If there are more than two cofounders, limit the team that's presenting to two people so you are efficient in using the time of the management team. I recommend that one person do at least 75 percent of the pitching so that there is consistency of voice and messaging. Develop a rudimentary question-and-answer document and decide among the founders who should respond to a specific question. The CEO should also be the point person to decide who should answer a specific question when you meet with the investors.

Once the VC firm has decided to invest in the firm, they will issue a term sheet within a few days. Once you accept the term sheet, it will take roughly thirty days to complete all the legal due diligence and negotiate the final legal documents. You should be prepared for the legal due diligence by working with your law firm to have all your legal documents (incorporation and prior financing documents, third-party contracts, employee/contractor agreements, previous investment documents, board meeting minutes, and so on) in a digital vault that the investor's law firm can easily access. Once the legal documents have been finalized and signed, the VC firm(s) will then release the funds to you, and you are ready to move on to the next phase of your company.

BUILDING A COMPELLING INVESTOR PITCH

O nce you have identified your target VC firms, it is time to develop your investor pitch. You should give yourself a good four to six weeks to develop your pitch, as it will take multiple iterations to put it together and get feedback from your team and existing investors in your company. A well-developed investor pitch can also serve as the foundation for your pitch to potential customers as well as potential employees for the company.

A typical investor pitch should be no more than twelve to fifteen slides. Your goal with the pitch is to stimulate interest in the company and to get the next meeting from the VC firm. It is not to provide every little detail about the company. As mentioned earlier, the VC firms will typically hold several meetings with the company to go into more details about the product, the technology architecture, and the traction before bringing you in front of the entire partnership.

The objective of a pitch is to demonstrate that you have a deep understanding of the problems facing your market, and you have a clear, long-term vision and a well-thought-through plan on how to tackle the problem space. VCs like to invest in smart people. You want to use the investor pitch to show that you are several steps ahead of the VCs in thinking through how you will win with your company.

Storytelling

One of the most important aspects of a pitch I try to understand is the founder's journey in starting their company. What is the founder's specific insight or experience with the target market that has allowed him or her to build a compelling solution for the market? As an example, I am an advisor to a company called Ally, which offers a SaaS solution for managing OKRs (objectives and key results). Prior to starting Ally, the founder had built his own internal solution using spreadsheets to manage OKRs at his previous company. However, he struggled to make this solution work effectively as spreadsheets were not the right platform for building this solution. He then built a custom application for managing OKRs, shared it with other founders, and got excellent feedback. His experience gave him the insight and the confidence to start a new company to commercialize the solution he had built. **As of October 2020, the company is growing rapidly and has raised more than $23 million in funding from top VC firms.**

Another aspect of storytelling is how you project the market opportunity to investors. It is not just a dry set of numbers regarding the potential TAM (total addressable market); rather it is a story about the trends sweeping your target market. In particular, you need to sell the investor on what changes are transpiring that make your solution ripe for the market. For example, in selling the vision around Livemocha in 2007, I described a world being swept by globalization, rapid adoption of broadband internet, and social networking solutions. It became relatively easy to convince investors that there would be billions of users who would turn to online language learning tools to learn English so they could get ahead in a globalized world.

What Are Venture Capitalists Looking for in a Pitch?

TEAM, TEAM, AND TEAM

Most VCs will tell you that the team is the most important criteria that they invest in. Largely, this is true for most investors, though they will take a bet on inexperienced founders when the idea and traction are compelling. Investors look for founders who have a deep understanding of the problem that they are trying to solve. Generally, this comes about because the founders come from the industry, bring deep expertise, and have experienced the problem themselves. They look for founders who are clearly passionate about the problem they are trying to solve and the company they are looking to build. They prefer to work with founders who have a growth mindset and are open to learning and feedback.

Investors also like to invest in a founding team as opposed to an individual founder (unless they are an exceptional entrepreneur). Two (or more) minds are always better than one. A single founder raises doubts in the minds of the investor about whether you have the capacity to convince others of your idea.

TRACTION

A key area of assessment for VCs is to understand whether the company has achieved product/market fit with its solution. The best way to demonstrate product/market fit is to show that your solution is hitting it on all cylinders in terms of user adoption, engagement, and revenues. For example, in the early days of Facebook, at Harvard, they had extraordinary user engagement with 65 percent daily active users and 95 percent monthly active users. The total user population was quite small, but it was clear that the Facebook team had achieved something magical with its solution.

MARKET SIZE

VCs like to invest in markets that are at least tens of billions of dollars in size. They want to see companies that can grow to at least $75 to $100 million in revenues over five to seven years. This means that the company can be valued in the billion-dollar-plus range when it goes public. With this kind of a valuation, a VC firm could achieve a cash-on-cash return of five to ten times, assuming that they own 25 percent of the company.

COMPETITIVE MOAT

VCs look for companies that can create an unfair competitive advantage over their competitors. They don't like to invest in companies that are in a crowded space, and the only competitive advantage is a few extra features. They like to invest in companies that are in industries being swept by significant market forces or disruptive technological changes. They look for companies that can establish significant network effects where it becomes a winner-take-all market. With AI/ML (artificial intelligence and machine learning) taking off, VCs are also increasingly looking for companies that have access to proprietary data sets that will allow these companies to develop unique machine learning models to solve industry-specific problems.

PITCH DECK OUTLINE

For the pitch deck outline, I like the business plan template[1] developed by Sequoia Capital. I have outlined a slightly modified version of the template below.

Company Purpose

This can also be your title slide. You should use this slide to provide an elevator pitch about what the company does. Outline what problem the company is solving and your key value proposition. Where possible, use an analogy to make the value proposition simple and easy for the audience to understand. For example, you could be "An Uber for after-school rides" or "An Airbnb for physical storage."

For Airbnb, its one-sentence tagline from its original pitch deck was "Book rooms with locals, rather than hotels."[2] From there, the pitch immediately jumps into a more detailed explanation of how price is an important consideration for travelers and how hotels leave travelers disconnected from the city and its culture.

LinkedIn's tagline from its Series B pitch was "Find and contact the people you need through the people you already trust."[3] While it is a longer statement of purpose, I find the tagline is easier to understand and conveys a stronger benefit in comparison to the Airbnb statement. The LinkedIn pitch follows up on the tagline by describing itself as People Search 2.0 and contrasting how People Search 2.0 differs from People Search 1.0 by leveraging people's network of relationships. To further illustrate the differences between 2.0 and 1.0 platforms, it gives other examples of online goods, payment platforms, and internet search, and how they have evolved in a similar fashion based on similar types of networks.

Problem

Describe the unmet problem that you are addressing and why it is important to address it. Specifically, outline the pain points that the target market is experiencing. Most VCs like to fund "aspirins, not vitamins," meaning that the customer has to be experiencing a pounding headache. Discuss why it matters that the problem be solved and how current solutions are inadequate. Outline the major industry trends or technology shifts that are causing this opportunity to emerge now.

As mentioned earlier, Ally is a company that helps enterprises of all sizes manage OKRs (objectives and key results). OKRs are a goal-setting framework developed by Andrew Grove, CEO of Intel, and later popularized by John Doerr, a legendary partner at Kleiner Perkins. OKRs have become a hugely popular methodology by which a number of companies are managing their employees and their execution priorities. In a hyper-competitive world, where the speed of business has increased dramatically, it has become more important for employee work to align with the objectives of the company. Millennials are also demanding increased transparency regarding the company's objectives. The OKR methodology requires that all OKRs, from top management to the lowest-level employees, be visible throughout the organization.

Companies have tried managing OKRs using spreadsheets. However, the problem is that spreadsheets are clunky tools to manage OKRs because it is difficult to clearly see the hierarchy of relationships between a manager's OKRs and her subordinates. As a result, more companies are looking to off-the-shelf, SaaS-based OKR management solutions like Ally to manage their company's OKRs.

Solution

Describe the solution that you have built and how it uniquely addresses the problem or pain points that you have identified. Make sure to describe your solution at a high level—don't get into the weeds of every feature that your solution includes. You will have an opportunity to go into a lot more detail when the VC firm organizes a follow-up meeting to do a technology deep dive. Detail any cost savings that your solution provides if appropriate and what kind of return on investment the customer will get.

Discuss the specific technical expertise that you bring to bear in developing the solution. Highlight the proprietary nature of the solution or the data you're utilizing or collecting.

Make sure that you put together a killer five-minute demo for your product. Where possible, do a live demo but have a backup video ready if your demo fails for any reason or you don't have a proper setup. Use a customer scenario to demonstrate the capabilities of the product as opposed to simply demonstrating the product features.

Traction

This is one of the most important slides in your presentation deck as it will demonstrate whether you have achieved product/market fit. Share charts showing growth in customers, daily and monthly active users, bookings, monthly or annual recurring revenues, conversion rate from free to paid customers, and so on. Show retention rates for a daily or weekly cohort of users. If you are an enterprise offering, show your pipeline of potential customers. If you have a freemium offering, show the conversion from free to paid customers and the churn rate of paying customers. Ideally, you want to show a rapidly growing trend in all these metrics.

When presenting annual recurring revenues, make sure that you are truly presenting annually recurring revenues. For example, if you have a contract that's paying you on a monthly basis but has a definitive end date, you cannot include it in your ARR calculation. You should only use monthly recurring revenues that have no end date. Finally, don't show cumulative metrics as that is a sure sign that you don't have strong month-by-month growth, and you are trying to hide it by showing cumulative numbers.

Market Opportunity

Describe the total addressable market (TAM) for your solution and how fast it is growing. Discuss the trends that are driving the overall growth in the market, especially why these trends create the opportunity for your solution now. Where possible, you should present industry data published by reputable market research firms like Gartner, Forrester Research, and so on. Make sure that your market is at least several billion dollars in size, otherwise the VC firms will not be interested. You should present both US market data as well as the international market opportunity.

Be prepared to share data about the revenues of existing players in the market as well. This will serve to validate the overall size of the market and provide a picture of how crowded it is.

Be careful about limiting yourself to the current industry size. Icertis is a leader in the contract management space. When it started in 2010, the total size of the contract management space was estimated to be only $300 million. Existing players in the market were at most $20 to $30 million in size. Looking at the market then, most VCs would have rejected the market opportunity as too small. However, Icertis redefined the market as one in which companies could extract information from the contract and unlock the value in these contracts. By redefining the market, they were able to dramatically grow the market, and today most analysts size the market as $20 billion in size.

Competition

This is another important slide, as the VC firms will try to understand how crowded your market is and if you have a clear, unfair competitive advantage that will allow you to win. You should outline the overall competitive landscape in the form of a 2x2 chart showing the different axes of competition (see Airbnb competitive matrix in Figure 3 from an early pitch deck). Pick axes that are meaningful from a competitive differentiation point of view. You should always show your company at the top right-hand side.

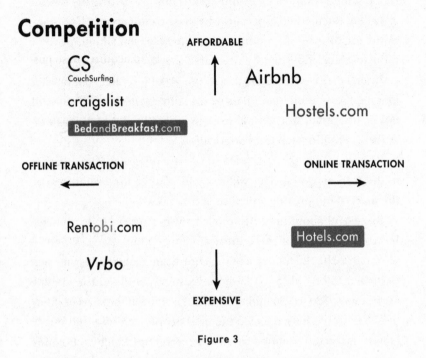

Figure 3

You should outline the secret sauce that will allow you to build an unfair competitive advantage that is difficult for the competition to replicate. Network effects are a great example of a competitive advantage that is very hard for competitors to overcome. I love marketplace companies such as OfferUp, Poshmark, and so on, as a growing installed base leads to network effects that create a significant moat for these companies. If you are leveraging AI/ML to build your solution, having access to proprietary data can also be a significant competitive advantage.

I am not a big fan of feature comparison lists. It simply highlights that you have some temporary competitive advantage based on a few features. It is not going to give the VCs a sense that you have a clear, sustainable, competitive advantage that will allow you to win over your competitors in the long term.

Go-to-Market Strategy

In this section, you should start by discussing the type of customer you plan to target and how you are planning to acquire these customers. You should discuss if there are customer segments that you are specifically targeting. Initially, I highly recommend focusing on a narrow customer segment, as your marketing messaging can be targeted to the unmet needs of your target customer segment. Your product feature set should also be highly tuned to address the needs of your target segments. Once you have successfully penetrated a specific customer segment, you can expand to other customer segments. Facebook is a great example of a highly targeted customer segment focus at its inception. Mark Zuckerberg started by offering his service only to Harvard students. Once he had successfully penetrated Harvard, he expanded to other universities and eventually opened up the solution to consumers at large.

If you are targeting enterprise customers, you might target by customer size—for example, small businesses versus Fortune 1000 (F1000) customers or by specific vertical. The marketing and sales strategy that you utilize to target small businesses will be very different from those that you use to target large enterprises. For example, to target small businesses, you might look at a combination of web advertising, SEM (search engine marketing), and insider sales to address this market. For large enterprises, you may need a combination of web advertising, industry analyst PR, and a dedicated enterprise sales force to call on potential enterprise customers.

Ally, the SaaS tool for managing OKRs, started off by utilizing SEM to generate leads. These leads directed potential users to Ally's website where customers could sign up for a two-week free trial, after which they must pay to continue to use the service. The Ally sales team would then try to identify accounts that were departments within large enterprises and call on these accounts to get larger enterprise-wide deployments of its SaaS solution. As Ally has grown its marketing organization, it has invested in SEO (search engine optimization) to generate more leads that it can then utilize to pursue large account opportunities.

If you are targeting mid-size to large enterprise customers, you should show your current pipeline of customers at different stages of the sale as well as logos of prominent enterprise customers you have secured. This will provide the VCs greater comfort that you have an active sales effort and that you are having good success transitioning customers at different stages of the sales cycle.

Business Model

You should outline how you expect to generate revenues with your offering. If your basic offering is free, discuss whether you expect to make money through advertising or a paid version that has additional features. If you are planning to make money through advertising, you should discuss who you expect your advertisers to be, what is the value proposition for them to advertise on your site, what ad networks you plan to use, what you expect to charge advertisers, and whether it is a CPM (cost per mille), CPC (cost per click), or sponsorship model. You should provide proof points for what other, similar sites have charged for advertising on their sites.

If you have a freemium model, you should discuss what your experience has been in converting free customers to paid customers and the churn rate you are experiencing if it is a subscription offering. Your churn rate will have a big impact on the LTV (lifetime value) of your customer. Ideally, you should be converting 5 to 10 percent of your free customers to paid customers, and your churn rate should be less than 2 percent a month.

If you are using distribution channels to reach your customer, you should share the distribution fee or revenue share you have to pay to your distribution channel partner. It is not uncommon to have to pay 25 to 50 percent of your revenue as a distribution fee.

Finally, you should discuss your CAC (customer acquisition cost). The cost of customer acquisition that you should be measuring is the cost of acquiring your paid users, not just acquiring registered users. To calculate your CAC, you should only factor in the paid users whom you acquire through a paid acquisition program. Don't include organic customers who discover your solution on their own. Typically, VCs like to see a ratio of a minimum of 3:1 for LTV to CAC. Ideally, this ratio should be more like 5:1.

Team

In this section, you should outline the key members of the management team and their past experience. You should specifically outline if they have any prior expertise in the space you are targeting as well as any prior startup experience and success. Describe any major accomplishments—for example, successful exits, prior patents, successful product introductions, and so on. VCs also want to understand how you know the other cofounders and members of the management team and whether you have a history of working with one another.

If you have advisors who bring specific industry expertise or connections, list them as well, but only if they are actively involved in advising your startup. VCs will often ask if any of the advisors are investors in the company as that would further validate that your idea has merit. It is not a requirement that the advisors invest in the company; however, your story becomes a lot stronger if they are investors as well.

Financials

Most people make the mistake of developing detailed, five-year P&L (profit and loss statement) projections. The reality is that most

VCs will not spend time understanding your long-term projections because they don't believe it's possible to project long-term revenues with any accuracy. I, therefore, recommend sharing the P&L projections only up until the next fundraising milestone, which is typically twelve to twenty-four months, as you are likely to have better visibility on these projections.

Chris Janz, partner at Point Nine Capital, offers an excellent SaaS model that you can use to develop your business model. It has excellent charts that you can include in your business plan.[4]

In sharing P&L projections, discuss the key assumptions that went into developing the revenue projections. These assumptions should ideally be backed up by your current experience in marketing and selling your product. For example, if you are generating leads from an SEM campaign, discuss your CPC rate, your conversion to free trial, your conversion from free trial to paid customers, and so on. Similarly, discuss the key expense projections such as head count and marketing spend.

Note that, in the early years, VCs like to see revenue growth that is at least 200 to 300 percent a year. If you are raising seed funding, your investors want to make sure that you can achieve a $1 million ARR (annual recurring revenue) run rate by the time you are ready to raise your Series A funding round.

Ask

For this slide, you should provide your prior funding history and outline how much you want to raise for your next round. Ideally, you should propose a single number for the amount of money that you would like to raise as opposed to a range. This will convey that you have your act together as opposed to looking wishy-washy in terms of your requirements.

You should outline the use of funds—how much will go into product development, how much into marketing and sales, and so on. This should be consistent with the P&L that you have put together.

Unless it is purely an angel raise, don't outline the terms that you are seeking for the raise. You may be unnecessarily shortchanging yourself as competing term sheets may result in a higher valuation for your company. In any case, the size of your raise will give the VC an approximate idea of the valuation you are expecting for your company.

Appendix

As mentioned earlier, you should plan on having no more than twelve to fifteen slides in your pitch deck. This obviously does not allow you to provide the level of detail that might be needed to address any questions that come up. You should, therefore, include another five to seven slides in your appendix that you can pull up as needed. However, in the interest of maintaining the flow of the conversation during the meeting, make sure not to spend too much time on any specific detail. Suggest deferring an in-depth discussion to a follow-up meeting if the VC is interested in pursuing the discussion further.

The areas where you might want to create additional slides include detailed features, screenshots, and architecture for the product. Also consider having additional slides regarding the key metrics that you are tracking for your product, specifically cohort analysis displaying engagement and retention. Finally, you should be prepared to provide additional details around your competitors and how you stack up against them.

12

EARLY-STAGE FUNDING VEHICLES

Startups can raise funding either through the issuance of equity or debt. However, the "debt" that they raise is not your typical debt where you have to pay off the principal in monthly installments. It is essentially a form of future equity in the company that is issued in a subsequent financing of the company. The most common form of early-stage financing is a convertible note. Equity issuance can also come in various forms. The simplest form is called a SAFE, which is like a convertible note in many respects but avoids some of the drawbacks. More elaborate equity funding (also known as a preferred round) is typically done when raising a Series A or beyond, using a standard set of financing documents that can be a lot more expensive to execute.

In addition to equity, startups can also raise venture debt, which is like a traditional loan that you can get from a bank. You have to pay off the loan via monthly installments over a fixed period. In addition, the venture debt banks will also take a small amount of equity as warrants for the risk that they are taking. The key benefit of taking on venture debt is that you are avoiding significant dilution to your equity ownership. However, there's significant risk to taking on venture debt if you encounter difficult circumstances and are unable to pay off the loan.

CONVERTIBLE NOTE

A convertible note is the most common form of funding that startups use during the seed stage of funding. The main benefit of a convertible note is that it is relatively simple and inexpensive to implement compared to a full preferred equity round—typically costing $5,000 or so in legal fees. A full-fledged equity round of financing can cost $35,000 to $50,000 to execute, which can be prohibitive if you are raising less than $1 million in funding. There are also other inexpensive alternatives to equity funding such as a SAFE (simple agreement for future equity) and Series Seed that have become popular. I will discuss these other methods of funding following this section.

Key Terms

A convertible note is essentially a debt instrument with a provision for automatic conversion to equity when the startup executes an equity round typically in excess of $1 million. Here are some of the key terms of a convertible note:

PRINCIPAL

The principal is due only at the end of the term of the note (or upon bankruptcy) if there is no subsequent financing. Typically, the principal along with accrued interest is converted to equity upon a subsequent equity financing of a certain size (e.g., if the company is raising $1 million or more in funding).

INTEREST

The note earns an interest rate typically of 6 to 8 percent. However, the note simply accumulates interest—there is no payment of the interest to the note holder. The accumulated interest is added to the principal, which gets converted to equity upon a subsequent financing. Let's say that you raise a $100,000 convertible note at a 6 percent interest rate, and you raise a $1 million equity round after one year. At the end of one year, the investor's principal has increased to $106,000, which is the amount that would be converted to equity.

DISCOUNT

Typically, the principal (and accrued interest) will convert to equity at a 20 percent discount to the preferred share price of a subsequent equity round. For example, if the preferred share price is $5 in a future raise, investors get to convert their note investment at a share price of $4. I have also seen higher discounts or the provision for warrants if the company is not able to raise funding by a certain time. For example, you might see a provision that says that the discount increases to 30 percent if the company is unable to raise funding within two years. We typically don't see provisions these days for increases in the discount rate. The interest rate on the principal essentially acts like an additional discount that increases over time.

VALUATION CAP

Even with the discount, most notes include a valuation cap—for example, the valuation for the raise cannot exceed $5 million. Investors get the lower of the 20 percent discount or the valuation cap. For example, if the raise is at a $10 million valuation and note terms say that note investors get the lower of a 20 percent discount or a $5 million cap, then the note investors can convert their investment to equity at a $5 million valuation.

TERM

The term is typically one to two years. However, it is fairly easy to get permission from investors to extend the period if you are not able to execute a preferred equity round prior to the end of the term.

AUTOMATIC CONVERSION TO EQUITY

The note includes an automatic conversion to equity at a preferred equity raise greater than $1 million. The investors get most of the same terms as other investors in that round except for the valuation and other terms such as pro rata rights (the right to invest in future rounds), which is typically granted to larger investors only.

CHANGE OF CONTROL

If a change of control—for example, an acquisition—happens prior to conversion of the note into equity, then typically the note investor has a choice of getting a 50 to 100 percent premium on their investment or the option to convert to equity at the valuation cap specified in the note.

The Hidden Traps of Convertible Notes

We have talked about the benefits of a note—namely simplicity and cost. There are also typically no control provisions or requirement for board seats, though there is nothing preventing investors from asking for board seats. However, there are many downsides that you need to consider.

LACK OF VISIBILITY ON DILUTION

Since no shares are issued with a convertible note, a note doesn't show up in the capitalization table for the company. A capitalization table, or cap table, is simply a ledger of the equity ownership in a company. As a result, founders don't know how much dilution they have suffered with a note until a full preferred equity round is raised when the note is finally converted to equity. In addition, if the startup is not doing well, it will typically raise more money through additional notes, which begin to pile up. When the cap table is finally updated post a Series A raise, founders are typically quite surprised by how much equity they have given up.

SUPER LIQUIDATION PREFERENCE

Most preferred equity investors receive a 1x liquidation preference, which means that they receive all their money first before any common shareholders in the event of a sale. Even though note holders get equity at a discount to new investors in a preferred round, they receive the same per share liquidation preference as that of new investors who invest at a higher share price.

To understand how this works, let's take an example of a startup that's raised $1 million in a note at a valuation cap of $4 million. The company subsequently raises $10 million in Series A funding at a $20 million pre-money valuation. Let's assume that the company has 10 million shares prior to raising its equity round.

	Series A Investors	Note Investors
Investment	$10,000,000	$1,000,000
Valuation	$20,000,000	$4,000,000
Per share value	$20,000,000/ 10,000,00 = $2	$4,000,000/ 10,000,000 = $0.40
# of shares	$10,000,000/ $2 = 5,000,000	$1,000,000/ $0.40 = 2,500,000
Per share liquidation preference	$2	$2
Total liquidation preference	5,000,000 x $2 = $10,000,000	2,500,000 x $2 = $5,000,000

As you will see in this example, the note investors get the same per share liquidation preference as the Series A investor leading to a total liquidation preference that is five times their investment of $1 million. As a result of the higher preference that the note holders receive, the company has to be sold for more than $15 million before the common shareholders, including the founders, receive any money at all. There are two ways to get around this problem. The company could issue the note holders a combination of preferred and common shares so that their liquidation preference doesn't exceed $1 million in this example. Or, the company could issue a "shadow preferred stock" to the investors, which is identical to the Series A except that it has a lower liquidation preference per share.

"FULL-RATCHET-ANTI-DILUTION-LIKE" PROVISION

Most equity rounds today include what's called a "broad-based weighted average" anti-dilution provision. This means that if you raise a future round at a lower valuation, then existing investors get additional shares to compensate them for having invested previously at a higher valuation. However, the number of additional shares they get takes into account how much new funding you have raised. The goal is to lower the overall valuation for the existing investors so they are treated fairly compared to new investors.

With a note, however, by agreeing to a discount in a future round of funding, you are agreeing to essentially a "full ratchet" anti-dilution provision, which means that investors get to convert all the funds at the new valuation plus a 20 percent discount. Let's say you raised funding in the form of a note at a 20 percent discount and a $4 million valuation cap, and then later raise a full equity round at a $3 million valuation. The note holders will get converted at 80 percent of a $3 million valuation, or a $2.4 million valuation, which is a great deal for the note holders.

In reality, however, I think this is a moot issue. If you are unable to raise funding at higher valuation from the valuation cap that you have set for your note, it is highly unlikely that you will be able to raise any money at all.

POTENTIAL LOSS OF CONTROL UPON NONPAYMENT

If you are unable to raise equity funding before the term of the note ends and are unable to pay back the note holders, you are now at the mercy of the note holders. Most of the time, your note holders will allow you to extend the term of the note. However, there's a nonzero chance that they will force payment of the note. At that point, your primary fiduciary responsibility is to maximize payment to the note holders, which may force you to sell the IP of the company or sell the company before you are ready to do so.

In practice, however, I have not heard of any situation where founders have been forced into bankruptcy or have lost control of their company. Most of the time, the company simply shuts down once the founders have run out of options, and everyone simply moves on.

14

SAFE
(SIMPLE AGREEMENT
FOR FUTURE EQUITY)

A SAFE financing instrument, which was developed and popularized by Y Combinator,[1] avoids many of the pitfalls of a convertible note. Like a convertible note, a SAFE can have a valuation cap and a discount to the price of a future equity round. Unlike a note, the valuation cap used in a SAFE is a post-money valuation cap (as compared to convertible notes, which use pre-money valuation caps), allowing the amount of dilution suffered to be calculated exactly. A SAFE is also somewhat more cost efficient compared to a note given its simplicity. As a result, SAFEs are increasingly utilized instead of notes, especially in Silicon Valley.

Let's say that a founder initially raises $500,000 at a $5.5 million post-money cap. The dilution the founder would suffer is:

$500,000/$5.5 million = ~9 percent

Subsequently, the founder raises another $500,000 at an $8.3 million post-money cap. The dilution that the founder would suffer is:

$500,000/$8.3 million = ~6 percent

In total, the company would have suffered ~15 percent dilution by issuing the two SAFEs.

Here are the notable differences between a convertible note and a SAFE:

EQUITY VERSUS DEBT INSTRUMENT

A SAFE is intended to be an equity instrument compared to a note, which is a debt instrument with a convertible feature. It is essentially a warrant for future equity in the company. A SAFE has no maturity date and no interest rate. Given that it is not a debt instrument and has no maturity date, you don't risk nonpayment at maturity and being at the mercy of your investors, who can potentially force you into bankruptcy.

PRE-MONEY VERSUS POST-MONEY VALUATION CAP

With a note, the valuation cap is pre-money, whereas with the current form of a SAFE, the valuation cap is post-money. The advantage of having a post-money valuation cap is that both the investors and the founders know exactly how much dilution they have suffered through the SAFE, even if the company raises more capital with additional SAFEs in the future. However, the cost of dilution from future SAFEs is borne entirely by the founders. With a note, the exact dilution is not known until a future equity round is raised and existing note investors suffer dilution from future note investments.

Typically, even though the amount of dilution that the company suffers from a SAFE is known when it is issued, like a note, you don't usually see a SAFE showing up on the cap table. This is because the valuation of a future priced round could be lower than the valuation cap of the SAFE, in which case more shares will be issued to SAFE holders, and they will suffer even greater dilution.

NO "FREE" LIQUIDATION PREFERENCE

As discussed earlier, one issue with notes is the "free" liquidation preference—in other words, you can have a liquidation preference higher than the amount put in by note investors. With a SAFE, the amount invested converts to its own series of preferred stock with the amount of liquidation preference equal to the amount invested as a SAFE.

PRO-RATA RIGHTS

A SAFE provides for a side letter option that allows investors to get pro rata rights in a future financing. As an example, if an investor owns 20 percent of the company, he or she gets the right to invest 20 percent of a future round. Typically, you don't want to give this right to small investors who are common in seed financings. When VCs give you a term sheet for an investment, they typically want to invest the whole amount and don't like reducing their investment for smaller investors who have pro rata rights.

However, a SAFE has the same issue of including a Full Ratchet Anti-Dilution provision as a convertible note.

SERIES SEED FINANCING

As mentioned earlier, a convertible note or a SAFE won't show up on your cap table since no equity is actually issued. The alternative is to do a priced equity round where you issue preferred stock to investors at a specific valuation. However, a priced equity round has traditionally been quite expensive to execute, costing in the range of $35,000 to $50,000.

In 2010, lawyers from Fenwick & West started open sourcing a set of documents called Series Seed that make it considerably less expensive for startups to raise a priced equity round.[1] The documents used in a Series Seed financing typically have fewer terms compared to a traditional priced equity round. They only have two sets of documents—a Stock Investment Agreement and a Certificate of Incorporation. These days, many firms, including WSGR (Wilson

Sonsini Goodrich & Rosati), have their own set of updated Series Seed documents.

The key terms that Series Seed documents incorporate are:

- Liquidation preference—the right for investors to get their money first in the case of a liquidation or sale
- Limited protective provisions—prohibiting the company from taking certain actions without the consent of the preferred stockholders, such as changing rights of preferred stock, increasing authorized capitalization, creating senior series/class of preferred stock, redeeming stock, declaring dividends, changing board size, or selling or liquidating the company
- Board seat(s)
- Pro rata rights—major purchasers have the right to participate on a pro rata basis in subsequent financings
- Drag-along rights—if a majority of common shareholders, Series Seed shareholders, and the board approve a liquidation or sale of a company, then all shareholders have to vote in favor of the liquidation or sale of the company

What Series Seed documents do not include are:

- Anti-dilution protection—the right to get additional shares in a company if the company has a down round
- Registration rights—the right to register securities when the company goes public
- Right of first refusal and co-sale rights

Series Seed financings are increasingly used for financing under $1 million instead of a convertible note. They typically cost a little more than a convertible note to execute, generally in the range of

$10,000 to $15,000, depending on the number of investors and due diligence needed. The main benefit of a Series Seed financing is that the founders properly understand the dilution they are incurring with the financing, and this type of financing is a lot less expensive to execute compared to a full-priced round. I recommend that founders utilize Series Seed financing documents if they are raising between $500,000 to $2 million in financing.

Financing between $1 million and $2 million typically will utilize a full set of documents from the National Venture Capital Association, or NVCA (you may be surprised to hear that these are also referred to as Series Seed docs). The cost of executing a full set of documents can range from $35,000 to $50,000 because generally there are more terms to negotiate and more due diligence to conduct.

FINANCIAL PROVISIONS
IN A TERM SHEET

A term sheet is a document that investors put together to capture the key terms of their investment. Typically, once investors have decided to invest in a company, they issue a draft term sheet indicating their interest. Most of the terms of a VC term sheet are fairly standard—the main items that differ are the economic terms such as the amount of investment, the valuation at which the investment is being made, the price per share, the size of the option pool, and so on. It's important to carefully negotiate control provisions as well, especially details around the composition of the board of directors. The NVCA has a sample term sheet that outlines all the key terms in a typical investment.[1] I have also included a standard term sheet utilized by Wilson Sonsini Goodrich & Rosati, one of the top law firms in the business. In this chapter, we will discuss the financial terms and how they affect the dilution that you will face with any investment.

Preferred Shares

If you are raising an equity round, then you will need to issue "preferred" shares to your investors. Preferred shares are different from common shares that are issued to founders and employees. They have additional rights and preferences that the common shares don't have. These will be listed in more detail later in this chapter. As an example, preferred shares have the right to get their money first in the event of a liquidation or acquisition.

Valuation Concepts

To calculate the per share value of the shares that investors, and what equity stake they will receive, you need to understand the valuation that they place on your enterprise. The standard terms that are typically utilized for valuation in the industry are pre-money and post-money valuation. We will demystify these concepts.

PRE-MONEY VALUATION

Pre-money valuation is the valuation of your company when you are ready to raise your next round of funding. Your company's valuation is a function of the strength and completeness of your team, the amount of progress that you have made with your product, revenues you are generating, patents that your company may possess, and so on. This will be typically negotiated with investors when you go out and seek funding. In Seattle, for example, a strong team that has a product in market with a small amount of revenues can expect a valuation of between $5 to $10 million. In the Bay Area, the valuations are typically higher. Of course, the pre-money valuation cannot be mathematically calculated based on a multiple of revenue or earnings, like a public company, because most early-stage companies have little to no revenues, let alone positive earnings.

POST-MONEY VALUATION

Post-money valuation is the valuation of the company immediately after you raise funding. To calculate the post-money valuation, you add your funding amount to the pre-money valuation of the company. So, for example, if your pre-money valuation is $4 million and you raise $1 million in funding, your post-money valuation will be $4 million + $1 million = $5 million. Investors will now own $1 million/$5 million = 20 percent of your company, and the founding team and employees will now own 80 percent of the company.

Size of Option Pool

The amount of dilution that you suffer from an investment is not just a function of the pre-money valuation. Typically, investors will ask you to set aside between 15 and 20 percent of equity as an option pool with the percentage being calculated *post-funding*—in other words, after shares have been issued to the new investors. This way, the investors don't get further diluted whenever option grants are made to employees. The option pool has to be set aside first and is utilized in calculating the fully diluted number of shares that are authorized by the company. The fully diluted number not only includes all the common and preferred shares outstanding but also the number of options already granted, the size of your remaining available option pool, and any warrants that are outstanding.

Note that it is possible for you to negotiate the size of the option pool. The best way to do this is to create a budget for the number of options that you expect to grant until the next funding round. I was able to use this budget to negotiate a 12 percent option pool for one of my companies. However, make sure that you are not being too stingy in determining your budget, or you may not have enough options to grant to employees you would like to hire in the future.

Share Price Calculation

To calculate the share price at which you will sell your equity in the company, you need to divide the pre-money valuation that you have negotiated with investors by the fully diluted number of shares outstanding for the company. Let's consider a company that has a total of 10 million shares outstanding on a fully diluted basis that consists of 8 million common shares, 1 million in options granted, and 1 million in shares remaining in the option pool. Let's say that the investor asks for a 15 percent option pool post-funding and is willing to invest $5 million at a $15 million pre-money valuation. As a result of these terms, the company will need to expand its option pool by another 1.25 million shares. This is an iterative calculation so that you get to the 15 percent option pool post-funding. In this example, the company will have 11.25 million shares outstanding on a fully diluted basis instead of the earlier 10 million fully diluted number.

Share Price = $15 million/11.25 million shares = $1.33/share

The investor will now receive a total of $5 million/$1.33 shares, which equals 3.75 million shares for a 25 percent ownership in the company. Post-funding, there will be 11.25 million shares + 3.75 million shares = 15 million shares on a fully diluted basis. The option pool post-funding will be 2.25 million shares/15 million shares, which equals 15 percent of the fully diluted number of shares.

Liquidation Preference

While you might expect that in the case of a sale of the company the investors will receive proceeds proportional to their ownership interest, that is not always the case. Nearly always, the investors receive a "liquidation preference" in the case of a liquidation event (sale of the company or actual liquidation), which allows them to receive a full return of their investment (if not more) before the common stockholders receive any payout.

There are three types of liquidation preferences:

- Nonparticipating preferred stock: In this case, the investors receive only their investment back before the common stockholders receive any proceeds if they so choose. If it is in their interest, they can convert to common stock and receive the same per share return as all stockholders.

[ALTERNATIVE 1 (NONPARTICIPATING PREFERRED STOCK): First pay [one] times the original purchase price [plus accrued dividends] [plus declared and unpaid dividends] on each share of Series A Preferred (or, if greater, the amount that the Series A Preferred would receive on an as-converted basis). The balance of any proceeds shall be distributed pro rata to holders of common stock.]

- Fully participating preferred stock: In this case, the investors receive their investment back first and then receive their pro rata share of the remaining proceeds in proportion to their ownership. With a fully participating preferred stock, the investors will in all cases receive more money per share than holders of common stock.

[ALTERNATIVE 2 (FULLY PARTICIPATING PREFERRED STOCK): First pay [one] times the original purchase price [plus accrued dividends] [plus declared and unpaid dividends] on each share of Series A Preferred. Thereafter, the Series A Preferred participates with the common stock pro rata on an as-converted basis.]

- Participating preferred with a cap: This is similar to the fully participating option, except that the payout to the preferred investors is capped at a certain multiple of their investment.

[ALTERNATIVE 3 (CAP ON PREFERRED STOCK PARTICIPA-TION RIGHTS): First pay [one] times the original purchase price [plus accrued dividends] [plus declared and unpaid dividends] on each share of Series A Preferred. Thereafter, Series A Preferred participates with common stock pro rata on an as-converted basis until the holders of Series A Preferred receive an aggregate of [_____] times the original purchase price (including the amount paid pursuant to the preceding sentence).]

Let's take a look at a few examples of a sale of a company to see exactly how the proceeds from the sale would be distributed among common and preferred shareholders. Let's say that a VC has invested $5 million in a company at a $15 million pre-money valuation, which would mean that the VC owns 25 percent of the company. After a few years, the company is sold for $50 million.

- **Example 1:** Nonparticipating preferred stock with a 1x liquidation preference: The preferred shareholders would get their $5 million investment back first if they so choose. The common shareholders would receive a $45 million payout. In this case, the preferred shareholders would be better converting their shares to common stock and receiving a 25 percent payout, which would equal $12.5 million, and the common stockholders would

receive $37.5 million, directly proportional to their
ownership.

- **Example 2:** Fully participating preferred stock with a 1x
  liquidation preference: The preferred shareholders will
  receive $5 million back first. Then they would receive 25
  percent or an additional $11.25 million of the remaining
  $45 million in proceeds. In total, the preferred
  shareholders would receive $16.25 million in proceeds,
  and the common stockholders would receive the
  remaining $33.75 million.
- **Example 3:** Participating preferred with a 1x liquidation
  preference and a 2x cap on the participation. The
  preferred shareholder will receive $5 million back first,
  followed by 25 percent of the remaining proceeds up to a
  total of a 2x cap, or $10 million in total. In this case, the
  preferred shareholders would be better converting their
  shares to common stock and receiving a 25 percent
  payout, which would equal $12.5 million.

You can see that, with liquidation preferences, in the case of a
low-value sale, as a founder, you will likely not get a payout proportional to your equity ownership. Fortunately, most VC financings
use a nonparticipating preferred, so if the company has a successful exit, the preferred will convert to common, and the stockholders will share the proceeds based on their percentage ownership of
the company.

Dividends

A dividend is a payment of the profits of the business to the company's stockholders. The dividend provision can have a dramatic
economic impact on the eventual payments to the company's

founders, depending on how it's written. A "cumulative" dividend adds up over time and is paid out at the time of a liquidity event. A "noncumulative" dividend doesn't add up over time and is essentially meaningless, since there would be no dividend to pay out when the company is sold. It's very important from the founders' perspective to negotiate a noncumulative dividend because a cumulative dividend effectively increases the liquidation preference that is payable first to the investors.

> **DIVIDENDS:** Noncumulative dividends at an annual rate of 8 percent of the purchase price per share in preference to the common stock, when and if declared by the board. Any dividends in excess of the preference will be paid to the common stock.

Redemption Rights

In the current market, most term sheets don't provide for redemption rights. Redemption rights allow the VCs to get their money back after a certain time. Investors will sometimes include a redemption right in order to ensure that they get a return on their investment without waiting too many years. The redemption provision allows investors to cash out their investment when the company hasn't been able (or hasn't chosen) to sell or go public.

> **REDEMPTION RIGHTS:** Unless prohibited by Delaware law governing distributions to stockholders, the Series A Preferred shall be redeemable at the option of holders of at least [__] percent of the Series A Preferred commencing any time after [_____] at a price equal to the original purchase price [plus all accrued but unpaid dividends]. Redemption shall occur in three equal annual portions. Upon a redemption request from the holders of the required percentage of the Series A Preferred, all Series A Preferred

shares shall be redeemed (except for any Series A holders who affirmatively opt out).

Conversion/Automatic Conversion

Any investor has the right to convert his or her preferred shares into common shares at any time. Most investors will not convert to common unless they are forced to do so. More important is the provision for automatic conversion. The automatic conversion happens upon a qualified IPO or if 50 percent (or a specific percentage) of all preferred shareholders vote to convert to common. It is customary to have only common shares on the cap table when the company goes public because institutional investors don't like to see shares with rights that are greater than theirs.

The other scenario in which investors will convert their preferred shares to common is in a "cramdown" situation (a financing where existing nonparticipating investors suffer significant dilution) where the company is doing poorly and has to raise money at a lower price per share than previous financings. In that situation, the new investors typically want to eliminate the accumulated liquidation preference that investors have piled on the company over multiple rounds, leaving very little potential upside for the management team. By converting all existing preferred shares into common stock, the company starts with a clean cap table that provides enough incentive for the management team and employees to stay with the company and work toward its long-term success.

CONVERSION: The preferred may be converted at any time, at the option of the holder, into shares of common stock. The conversion rate will initially be 1:1, subject to anti-dilution and other customary adjustments.

ANTI-DILUTION PROVISION

The anti-dilution provision protects investors from situations where future investors invest at a valuation lower than the price per share paid by existing investors. There are essentially two ways that this can be done: full ratchet or a weighted average option. With a full ratchet option, the investors' conversion price to common is reduced as if the earlier investors had invested at the new share price. The weighted average anti-dilution option is the industry standard and is much more favorable to the common stock because it makes a smaller adjustment than the full ratchet, based on how much lower the price per share of the new round is and the number of shares issued at the lower valuation.

In the event that the company issues additional securities at a purchase price less than the current Series A Preferred conversion price, such conversion price shall be adjusted in accordance with the following formula:

ALTERNATIVE 1: "Typical" weighted average:

CP2 = CP1 * (A+B) / (A+C)

CP2 = Series A conversion price in effect immediately after new issue

CP1 = Series A conversion price in effect immediately prior to new issue

A = Number of shares of common stock deemed to be outstanding immediately prior to new issue (includes all shares of outstanding common stock, all shares of outstanding preferred stock on an as-converted basis, and all outstanding options on an as-exercised basis; and does not include any convertible securities converting into this round of financing)

B = Aggregate consideration received by the corporation with respect to the new issue divided by CP1

C = Number of shares of stock issued in the subject transaction

The following issuances shall not trigger anti-dilution adjustment:

(i) securities issuable upon conversion of any of the Series A Preferred, or as a dividend or distribution on the Series A Preferred; (ii) securities issued upon the conversion of any debenture, warrant, option, or other convertible security; (iii) common stock issuable upon a stock split, stock dividend, or any subdivision of shares of common stock; and (iv) shares of common stock (or options to purchase such shares of common stock) issued or issuable to employees or directors of, or consultants to, the company pursuant to any plan approved by the company's board of directors [including at least [_____] Series A director(s)].

CONTROL PROVISIONS
IN A TERM SHEET

n chapter 16, I describe the main economic provisions of a term sheet that are often the most heavily negotiated. The rest of the terms that you will find in a term sheet are fairly boilerplate and are typically not negotiated with investors, except around the edges. These terms protect the interests of investors and sometimes give them outsized control over the operations and destiny of the company. Most important, investors will have the ability to block a sale of the company or a future financing, even if they don't have a majority ownership in the company.

• • •

Board of Directors

The term sheet will typically outline the total size of the board, the number of board members who can be selected by the common shareholders, and the number of board members who can be selected by the preferred shareholders. Often, for more mature companies, there will also be provision for an independent board member who is selected by both common and preferred shareholders.

Typically, after a seed financing, the company will have three board members—two board members designated by the common shareholders (typically founders) and one board member designated by the investors. It is important that the board member representing the investors understands he or she will stay on the board only until a Series A financing is completed. At that point, the new investors will want board representation.

After a Series A financing, the board will typically have five board members—two designated by the common shareholders, two designated by the investors, and one independent board member. One of the board members designated by the common shareholders is reserved for the current CEO. Note that if the company hires a new CEO, the founders would effectively lose a board seat, depending on how the provision is written. It is important that you do proper due diligence on the investors and specifically the people who will be on your board. I highly recommend that you get VC board members who have been successful entrepreneurs themselves, if not operators. They are much more likely to understand how difficult it is to build a successful startup and will have valuable advice to offer as you grow your company.

THE INDEPENDENT BOARD MEMBER

The selection of the independent board member should be made carefully. You should ideally select someone who is local, has relevant industry expertise, is an operator or a successful entrepreneur, and has time to commit to board meetings. It is also important that you drive the process of selecting the independent board member. I had a situation where the VCs drove this process, and even though we were involved in selecting the independent board member, we found this person to be ultimately beholden to the interests of our VCs.

You will also need to compensate the independent board member with equity (it is extremely rare for private companies to pay cash compensation to board members). Typically, you would offer them options to purchase 0.25 to 0.5 percent of the company's fully diluted shares vesting over four years. Typically, board members designated by the investors do not receive cash or equity compensation for their service on the board.

BOARD OBSERVERS

You will likely encounter situations where investors will request observer seats on your board. This could be an associate or principal at the firm or a smaller investor or a strategic investor who doesn't want a formal board seat. I generally recommend that you avoid adding board observers as it can change the dynamics of the board even when the observer has no voting power. In any contentious discussion, you may feel that there are more people stacked against you as a result.

However, it is not always possible to refuse the request for an independent board observer as it sounds quite innocuous. In that situation, make sure that the addition of a board observer is done via a verbal agreement, and it is not captured in the financing documents.

ROLE OF THE BOARD

It is important to understand the governance role played by the board and how it is different from management. Typically, a board will have the following primary responsibilities:

- Hiring/firing the CEO
- Executive compensation, option grants
- Fundraising, mergers and acquisitions (M&A), debt issuance
- Strategy, performance/progress, financial review
- Approval of major third-party deals

Protective Provisions

Protective provisions are provisions that allow preferred shareholders to veto key corporate actions. Essentially, as long as the company has preferred shareholders (or a certain number of preferred shares), the company cannot take any of the following actions without written consent of a percentage of preferred shares. It is important that all preferred shareholders across different classes vote together as a group. Otherwise, you will give holders of a specific class veto rights over a specific corporate action. However, in late-stage funding scenarios, it is not uncommon for these investors to ask for certain rights (e.g., approval to sell the company) as their financial incentives may be very different from early-stage investors who could gain a lot from the sale of the company compared to late-stage investors. You will need to carefully negotiate the required votes and understand which stockholders you will need to obtain approval from.

Here are the typical corporate actions that would require approval from the preferred shareholders:

- Alter the rights and preferences of the preferred shares
- Liquidate or sell the company
- Amend the Certificate of Incorporation or company bylaws
- Create a series of shares that have preferences that are senior to the current preferred shares; essentially, this

means that the current investors have a veto right on future financings of the company

- Pay or declare dividends
- Borrow money that would increase the company's indebtedness beyond a certain amount
- Buyback any common stock
- Change the size of the board

Here's a list of typical protective provisions:

PROTECTIVE PROVISIONS: So long as at least 10 percent of the originally issued preferred shares is outstanding, consent of the holders of at least 50 percent of the preferred will be required for any action that (i) alters any provision of the Certificate of Incorporation or the bylaws if it would adversely alter the rights, preferences, privileges, or powers of, or restrictions on the preferred stock or any series of preferred; (ii) changes the authorized number of shares of preferred stock or any series of preferred; (iii) authorizes or creates any new class or series of shares having rights, preferences, or privileges with respect to dividends or liquidation senior to or on a parity with the preferred or having voting rights other than those granted to the preferred stock generally; (iv) approves any merger, sale of assets, or other corporate reorganization or acquisition; (v) approves the purchase, redemption, or other acquisition of any common stock of the company, other than repurchases pursuant to stock restriction agreements approved by the board upon termination of a consultant, director, or employee; (vi) declares or pays any dividend or distribution with respect to the common stock; (vii) approves the liquidation or dissolution of the company; (viii) increases the size of the board; (ix) encumbers or grants a security interest in all or substantially all of the assets of the company in connection with an indebtedness of the company; (x) acquires a material amount of assets through a merger or purchase of all or substantially all of the assets or capital stock of another entity; or (xi) increases the number of shares authorized for issuance under any existing stock or option plan or creates any new stock or option plan.

Information Rights

This term requires the company to deliver to investors an annual budget as well as audited yearly financials and unaudited quarterly financials. In addition, the company has to issue a report comparing the financial statements to the annual budget. It is fairly standard for investors to receive statements that show how the company is doing financially. Note that an annual audit can cost your company between $25,000 and $30,000 per year or more.

Registration Rights

Registrations rights allow the investors to sell their securities in the public market in the company's IPO and after the IPO. In order to sell any shares that the investors purchased before the IPO, in most cases, those shares first have to be registered with the federal government. The term sheet, therefore, includes provisions for both demand registrations and piggyback registrations. The investors can either "demand" a registration independent of any public financing activity, or they can "piggyback" on any financing the company is planning. In reality, the company and its underwriters have to be amenable to the timing of these registrations. In addition, during an IPO and for the following 180 days, the underwriters for the company's IPO will require that investors not sell their shares in order to avoid market disruptions.

REGISTRATION RIGHTS: *Registrable Securities.* The common stock issued or issuable upon conversion of the preferred stock will be "Registrable Securities."

DEMAND REGISTRATION. Subject to customary exceptions, holders of at least 50 percent of the Registrable Securities will be entitled to demand that the company effect up to two registrations (provided that each such registration has an offering price of at least $10 per share with aggregate proceeds of at least $20 million) at any time following the earlier of (i) five years following the closing of the financing and (ii) 180 days following the company's initial public offering. The company will have the right to delay such registration under certain circumstances for up to two periods of up to ninety days each in any twelve-month period.

PIGGYBACK REGISTRATION. The holders of Registrable Securities will be entitled to piggyback registration rights on any registered offering by the company on its own behalf or on behalf of selling stockholders, subject to customary exceptions. In an underwritten offering, the managing underwriters will have the right, in the event of marketing limitations, to limit the number of Registrable Securities included in the offering, provided that, in an offering other than the initial public offering, the Registrable Securities may not be limited to less than 25 percent of the total offering. In the event of such marketing limitations, each holder of Registrable Securities will have the right to include shares on a pro rata basis as among all such holders and to include shares in preference to any other holders of common stock.

S-3 RIGHTS. Subject to customary exceptions, holders of Registrable Securities will be entitled to an unlimited number of demand registrations on Form S-3 (if available to the company) so long as those registered offerings are each for common stock having an aggregate offering price of not less than $1 million. The company will not be required to file more than two such Form S-3 registration statements in any twelve-month period.

EXPENSES. Subject to customary exceptions, the company will bear the registration expenses (exclusive of underwriting discounts and commissions) of all demand, piggyback, and S-3 registrations, provided that the company will not be required to pay the fees of more than one counsel to all holders of Registrable Securities.

TERMINATION. The registration rights of a holder of Registrable Securities will terminate on the earlier of (i) such date, on or after the company's initial public offering, on which such holder may immediately sell all shares of its Registrable Securities under Rule 144 during any ninety-day period and (ii) three years after the initial public offering.

MARKET STANDOFF. Holders of Registrable Securities will agree not to effect any transactions with respect to any of the company's securities within 180 days following the company's initial public offering, provided that all officers, directors, and 1 percent stockholders of the company are similarly bound.

OTHER PROVISIONS. The Investor Rights Agreement will contain such other provisions with respect to registration rights as are customary, including with respect to indemnification, underwriting arrangements, and restrictions on the grant of future registration rights.

Pro Rata Investment Rights

A pro rata investment right gives investors the right to invest in a future investment in proportion to their ownership stake in the company. For example, if an investor owns a 20 percent stake in a company on a fully diluted basis, then they have the right to invest 20 percent in a future financing in the company. By doing this, the investor maintains the same stake in the company and avoids being diluted.

> **RIGHT TO MAINTAIN PROPORTIONATE OWNERSHIP:** Each holder of at least [500,000] shares of preferred will have a right to purchase its pro rata share of any offering of new securities by the company, subject to customary exceptions. The pro rata share will be based on the ratio of (x) the number of shares of preferred held by such holder (on an as-converted basis) to (y) the company's outstanding shares, options, and warrants (on an as-converted basis). Participating holders will have the right to purchase, on a pro rata basis, any shares as to which eligible holders do not exercise their rights. This right will terminate immediately prior to the company's initial public offering.

This is a right that you should only offer to major shareholders, which is generally anyone who has invested more than $250,000 in the company. Otherwise, it can be a real challenge to track down every investor to allow each to make an investment decision. Of course, as the size of each subsequent financing increases, it becomes increasingly challenging for angel investors to invest their pro rata share.

Sometimes VCs will ask for super pro rata rights, especially when they are investing in a small seed round. Essentially, they want to have the option to either lead the next round or get a larger stake in the company if it is doing really well. However, for entrepreneurs, it's a bad idea to give investors super pro rata rights because that makes it difficult for new investors to lead the round—they may not get enough stake in the company to make it worthwhile for them to invest. In addition, if the company is performing merely adequately (but not great) and VCs don't take advantage of their super pro rata right, that can send a bad signal to other investors who may be looking to invest in the company.

Drag-Along Rights

Drag-along rights give the larger shareholders the right to force all shareholders to vote their shares in favor of a merger or sale of the company. This provision is designed to prevent small shareholders from creating obstacles to a sale of the company, even if they don't have blocking rights. It is important to negotiate what stockholder vote is required to trigger the drag-along. If the preferred shareholders alone can force the drag-along, they can force the sale of the company, even over the objections of the common shareholders.

This right typically becomes an issue when a company has raised a lot of money but is failing and the investors want to sell the company at below the total liquidation preference. In this situation, the founders would not receive any consideration from the sale. The investors typically address this issue by carving out a certain percentage of the proceeds for the founders.

"DRAG-ALONG" RIGHT: Subject to customary exceptions, if holders of 50 percent of the preferred and 50 percent of the common stock approve a proposed sale of the company to a third party (whether structured as a merger, reorganization, asset sale, or otherwise), each stockholder will agree to approve the proposed sale. This right will terminate upon a Qualified Public Offering.

I am not in favor of having this provision in the term sheet unless the common shareholders also get to vote on the sale. Otherwise, it gives the investors too much power to force the sale of the company when the founders may not be ready to sell.

Right of First Refusal/Co-sale Right

The right of first refusal gives the company and, thereafter, investors the right to purchase any shares that the founders were planning to sell. Alternatively, they could choose to sell their shares on a pro rata basis along with the founders. The primary goal of this term is to limit the ability of founders to sell their shares and, therefore, align their interests with those of the investors and to limit the shareholder base of the company. These rights are completely standard in a term sheet.

> **RIGHT OF FIRST REFUSAL AND CO-SALE AGREEMENT:** In the event any founder proposes to transfer any company shares, the company will have a right of first refusal to purchase the shares on the same terms as the proposed transfer.
>
> If the company does not exercise its right of first refusal, holders of preferred stock will have a right of first refusal (on a pro rata basis among holders of preferred) with respect to the proposed transfer. Rights to purchase any unsubscribed shares will be reallocated pro rata among the other eligible holders of preferred.
>
> To the extent the rights of first refusal are not exercised, the holders of preferred stock will have the right to participate in the proposed transfer on a pro rata basis (as among the transferee and the holders of preferred stock).
>
> The right of first refusal and co-sale rights will be subject to customary exceptions and will terminate on an initial public offering.

CROWDFUNDING

The concept of internet-based product crowdfunding was popularized by Kickstarter (launched in 2009) and Indiegogo (launched in 2008). By 2020, of the two platforms, Kickstarter is the more popular platform. As of December 2019, Kickstarter had received more than $4.6 billion in pledges from 17.2 million backers to fund 445,000 projects in categories including films, music, stage shows, comics, journalism, video games, technology, publishing, and food-related projects. The average success rate for projects on Kickstarter is 37.5 percent. "Success" here is defined as achieving the minimum funding goal established for a project. The success rate for technology projects is lower—generally only one out of five projects gets funded.

From the perspective of a tech company, Kickstarter is a viable option to fund startups that are planning to develop video games and hardware. The founders of the Pebble watch, for example, raised more than $20 million in funding in 2015. Seattle-based Glowforge broke that record raising $27.9 million for its 3D laser printer also in 2015. For a time, it seemed like Crowdfunding platforms would disrupt the traditional angel/VC funding model—however, that has not turned out to be the case. In limited situations, for massively popular ideas, it can serve to jump-start a limited number of startups. However, it is no substitute for traditional fundraising. Even companies like Glowforge have turned to VC firms like the Foundry Group and True Ventures to fund their company.

To raise funds on Kickstarter, you need to create a project, and then set a deadline and a minimum funding goal. With Kickstarter, it is all or nothing. In other words, you get no funding if you don't hit the minimum goal that you have set for your project. Kickstarter takes a 5 percent fee for a successful project and charges another 3 to 5 percent for payment processing fees.

Platform Selection

You have a choice to host your project on Kickstarter, Indiegogo, or a self-hosted platform. Indiegogo has a flexible funding option where you can receive funds even if you don't meet your goal. However, I don't recommend this option, as you will be obliged to meet your reward obligations even if you don't get enough funds to complete your project. Also, you will get fewer backers, because potential backers will be concerned that you will not raise sufficient funds to fulfill your obligations.

You could explore the option of employing a self-hosted platform that you can integrate with your website. With a self-hosted platform, you don't have to wait to get your project approved or pay the 5 percent fee. You also control the experience in terms of communicating with your backers. However, you have to do all the heavy lifting to attract backers to your platform. All in all, Kickstarter is still your best option to promote your project because it has a large, built-in community that you can leverage; it is worth paying the 5 percent fee for the access to their community. You could also consider launching on both Kickstarter and Indiegogo so you gain access to both sets of communities and increase the amount of money that you raise for your product. I know of a company that launched initially on Kickstarter and, after their campaign was over, they launched on Indiegogo as well. With Indiegogo, one of the benefits is that you can continue to accept orders after your campaign is over.

Setting Your Goal

Set your goal at the minimum funding that you need to complete your project and fulfill the rewards that you have promised to your backers. Make sure to take into account all your development, manufacturing, payment processor and fulfillment, shipping costs, minimum order quantity, and so on. The lower the goal, the higher the likelihood of success. People love to back projects that have been oversubscribed. You get bragging rights about how you reached your goal in a short period or that you have raised X times your goal. This is likely to get you more PR that will further fuel interest in your project.

Messaging

It is important that you spend considerable time developing and refining your overall messaging for your project before you post it on a crowdfunding site. Create a document with your messaging and share it with friends and colleagues and get feedback.

A critical element of your story is a well-produced video. According to Kickstarter, "Projects with videos succeed at a much higher rate than those without (50 percent vs. 30 percent)." Consider hiring a professional production company to produce your video. Don't be afraid to spend at least $5,000 to produce your video. Obviously, you will have to make the initial investment and increase your goal, but it will be well worth it to compete effectively with other projects that are also vying for people's attention.

Rewards

Set your rewards to offer something unique that can incentivize backers to "buy" now as opposed to waiting for the product to launch. A key strategy for driving day one demand is to offer an early bird price for a limited number of units at a considerable discount off the retail price when the product is launched. Some people say that it is a bad idea to offer an early bird price because it may depress demand after the early bird promotion is over. Regardless, it is super important to drive day one demand. Make sure not to extend the early bird pricing too long as it can upset people who signed up early.

If possible, you should also offer a deluxe version of your product that is 25 to 50 percent more expensive than the base version and incentivizes people to spend a little more to get more goodies in their package. If you make the deluxe version too much more, most people will opt to go with the base version. This pricing strategy is not unlike the McDonald's Extra Value Meal pricing model where the entire meal is only a dollar more than just the burger. The goal is to entice you to pay a little more to get a soda and fries and make it seem like a great deal.

Marketing and Public Relations

A successful crowdfunding project starts even before the project is launched on the crowdfunding platform. You need to leverage the social media platforms where potential customers congregate to create the initial buzz for your offering. You can prompt their interest by creating an initial mailing list that you can reach out to when you finally launch your project. One of the ways to create a mailing list is to use Facebook ads or SEM (search engine marketing) to take users to a site that previews your offering. Collect their email addresses once they land on your site.

If you are a media savvy person with great contacts in the press, consider offering them an exclusive on your launch under embargo. If you can point to prior interest you have received and the mailing list that you have already built, it might create the interest for them to cover your launch. Be aware that the press is quite wary of writing about Kickstarter projects, given the number of scams and failures. The other option is to use PR post-launch once you have achieved two times or more in funding where you can point to your success in rapidly raising funding for your project.

It is super important to coordinate all your marketing efforts on day one of the campaign. Send out an email blast to your email list and coordinate all your social media promotion and advertising on day one of the campaign. If you can drive significant day one demand, it could catch the attention of the crowdsourcing platform, which might feature you as a result. It is estimated that 30 percent of all orders are placed on day one of a campaign.

VENTURE DEBT

Unlike convertible debt, which is a form of equity financing, venture debt is a form of debt financing that companies can use to fund themselves. Traditionally, companies utilize debt financing to extend their runway so they have more time either to meet key milestones or to achieve better financial results and, therefore, obtain a higher valuation for their next round of financing. Venture debt can also be utilized as a short-term bridge to the next round of financing. It is estimated that 25 to 30 percent of venture-funded companies use some form of venture debt financing. Typically, venture debt is available to companies after they have raised a seed or Series A round where there is validation from a major VC firm that the company has a viable future.

There are a number of players who offer venture debt including banks and venture debt funds. Among the banks, Silicon Valley Bank (SVB) is the most prominent player along with Square 1 Bank and Bridge Bank. Banks are generally more circumspect about their funding and are less expensive with respect to their loan terms. They operate across the spectrum from early-stage to late-stage financing. Venture funds, on the other hand, have a higher cost of capital, will take more risk with larger loans, and are, commensurately, more expensive with higher rates and higher warrant coverage. Venture funds are generally more focused on later-stage companies.

Banks like SVB will typically offer growth capital term loans that are 25 to 50 percent of the size of the prior VC financing round. In making the financing decision, the lender will look at a variety of factors, including the VCs that are backing the firm, the quality of the management team, the amount of capital that the company has raised, the company's growth, and prospects for raising the next round. The lender is essentially betting that the company will continue to be able to raise future financing rounds (or reach profitability) and pay off, or better yet, refinance its loan.

Banks like SVB also offer lines of credit based on accounts receivables or recurring revenue. Typically, these loans are for a twelve-month duration and may be renewed at the end of the twelve-month period. For an AR-based (accounts receivable) loan, you can expect to get a loan for 80 percent of the value of eligible accounts receivable (typically accounts receivable that are outstanding for fewer than ninety days). For a recurring-revenue-based loan, you can expect a loan for up to three times your monthly recurring revenues. Lines of credit are also generally somewhat cheaper than growth loans in terms of the interest rate charged because there is less risk to the bank in making these loans.

Most VCs recommend taking on venture debt mainly as a form of bridge financing to extend your runway in order to achieve certain milestones before raising the next round of financing. The other scenario is one where you have received a term sheet for the next round of financing but need additional funding to provide time to close the round. Under no circumstances should you draw down on the loan to extend your runway when it's clear that there is no hope of raising funding or selling your company. Your VC firm will not want to be on the hook if your company goes under after taking a loan. While they don't have an obligation to pay your loan, it makes it much harder for the VC firm to secure venture debt for other companies in its portfolio.

Financing Terms

Generally, the total length of the term loan is forty-eight months, including a drawdown period. The drawdown period is typically six to twelve months, which is the period you have to draw on the loan once you have signed the loan documents. This is also typically the period for interest-only payments. For example, if the drawdown period is twelve months and you draw down the loan after six months, you get six months of interest-only payments. Once the loan is drawn down and the interest-only period is over, the loan is amortized in a straight line over thirty-six months. Generally, you don't want to wait until the last minute to draw down on the loan, especially if you are running out of money. There is some risk that you may be denied the loan if the venture debt firm feels that there is no chance of payback.

The interest rate is set on a floating rate basis, so you are taking a risk that rates may go up in the future. The banks will typically be set at prime plus a spread that is generally between 0.5 and 2 percent. However, venture debt funds can be a lot more expensive. Their interest rates can vary between 18 and 30 percent, especially if they ask for no warrant coverage in return (though most ask for warrant coverage).

Another element of a bank's return are warrants that they use to juice up their overall return. The warrant coverage can be expressed as a percentage of the term loan commitment amount—for example, 2 percent coverage of a term loan commitment amount of $2 million, or $40,000 worth of warrants. Alternatively, it can also be stated as a percentage of the total equity on a fully diluted basis. In the latter case, the warrant coverage is generally between 0.2 and 0.3 percent of the total equity.

The next element of the warrant negotiation is whether the warrants are preferred or common stock warrants and the term of the warrant. In the past, banks generally insisted on preferred stock warrants, as they provide better price protection because of the anti-dilution protection they offer. However, these days, banks are increasingly going with common warrants because the strike price (the price at which an option or warrant can be exercised) is less expensive compared to a preferred stock warrant. Generally, the term is set to seven to ten years so that the banks are not forced to purchase the warrants before the company has a liquidity event. The final element of the warrant pricing is the strike price for the warrant. If the warrant is a preferred stock warrant, the price can be set either to the preferred stock price at the prior financing round or a future financing round. Generally, banks will insist on the former because the price of the preferred stock is a known quantity, and it is possible that the company may never have another financing round. If the warrant is a common stock warrant, the strike price will be equal to the price of the common stock at the last 409A valuation.

The pricing of the term loan is also affected by the loan origination fees that are assessed either upon closing or upon drawdown. It is in your interest, of course, to negotiate for the latter. Venture loan origination fees are generally in the 0.25 to 0.75 percent range, which is generally lower than the fees for traditional bank loans.

Covenants

Unlike traditional bank loans, growth capital loans to early-stage companies are characterized by a lack of financial covenants. The highly uncertain nature of early-stage companies makes it imprudent to put financial covenants in place. Most investors would be loath to allow their companies to take on venture debt with any kind of financial covenants.

While a growth term loan will not include any specific financial covenants, it will typically include terms that are categorized as affirmative or negative covenants. Examples of affirmative covenants include regulatory compliance, financial reporting, tax payments, and IP registration. Examples of negative covenants include restrictions on disposition of assets, change in control, additional indebtedness, and dividend distribution.

A key control term that all lenders will insist on is the material adverse change (MAC) clause, which refers to an adverse material change in the business or financial condition of the company. No material adverse change in the business should happen prior to the company drawing down on its loan. This is a clause that can cause startup CEOs a lot of heartburn, as there is legitimate fear that even if the loan gets funded that the bank could sweep the cash in their account to pay back the loan just when the loan is most needed by the startup. This is where it is essential to do proper due diligence on the bank to understand how inclined it is to invoke the MAC clause when the going gets tough. When I discussed this issue with a bank I am familiar with, I was told that to invoke the MAC clause, the bank needs to get the permission of the CEO, which is very difficult to get. Banks also want to maintain good relationships with the investors behind the early-stage startups, and they don't want to do anything to jeopardize those relationships.

A final control provision is the type of security interest that exists on the borrower's IP. Typically, this is expressed as a negative pledge where the bank does not get a lien on the company's IP but the company pledges not to provide an IP lien to any other entity.

PART IV

RUNNING YOUR COMPANY

RECRUITING
GREAT EMPLOYEES

Recruiting and retaining great employees is essential for any startup to be successful. However, it has become a tremendous challenge in the last decade because compensation at major companies like Microsoft, Facebook, Google, and others has sky-rocketed. You have to create a significant amount of buzz for your company and show meaningful traction in order to attract high-quality employees. The best candidates are never on the market, which means that you have to develop a strategy to attract these candidates to consider your startup. Once you have the opportunity to interview the superstar employees, you need to wow them with a compelling vision for the company. You have to demonstrate not only why your company would be a great place to work but also that you have a legitimate chance to achieve an IPO in the foreseeable future.

Start with a Great LinkedIn Profile

The first thing that any potential employee is going to do when contacted is to look up the LinkedIn profile of the founders. Make sure, therefore, to invest the time to thoroughly spruce up your LinkedIn profile so you can impress potential employees. List all your key accomplishments, prior startup work, and any patents that you may have filed. Ask your prior coworkers to write recommendations about you. In fact, you should guide them on the key points that you want to highlight so that people get an accurate perspective of what you are like to work with.

In addition to the founder profiles, create a profile about your company. If you have received funding from prominent angel or seed investors, make sure to mention this as it will give the company additional credibility. Share any articles that have been written about you in the press.

Take the time to invest in writing articles on LinkedIn and Medium that provide a perspective about trends in your industry as well as about your vision for the company. Make regular posts outlining the progress that you are making with your company.

Hiring Through LinkedIn

LinkedIn can be a great resource to identify and recruit potential employees. You can do a lot of personalized recruiting on LinkedIn in addition to placing ads on the platform. However, don't just leave it to an in-house human resources person or recruiter to contact potential recruits. Have them identify strong candidates who are a good fit based on your job description. Instead of the recruiter or an office admin contacting the candidate, you should reach out directly from your LinkedIn account. I have had great success in contacting potential recruits and hiring employees through this direct contact method. First, send the candidate a connection request over LinkedIn, which most people tend to accept. After they have accepted your connection request, you can contact them over email to let them know about the opportunity at your company. Suggest a meeting over coffee—it might be easier to accept that request as opposed to an interview at the company.

Hire Great Leaders

You can make your recruiting job a lot easier if you can hire great leaders who can bring their former team members with them. This strategy worked really well for us at TeamOn and Livemocha. At TeamOn, we hired a vice president of engineering who brought a number of his former engineers with him to the company (we hired four engineers this way). At Livemocha, we used the connections of one of my cofounders at his previous company to hire employees (until we got a cease-and-desist letter!). One way to determine if someone can bring his or her former team members is to ask for references of people who have worked for this person. You can do a reference check to see how they are viewed by people who have worked for this person as well as get a sense for their recruiting skills. Be aware, however, of any non-solicitation clause that might restrict your management team from hiring people away from their current positions.

Build the Founding Team

The first four or five hires for your company are some of the most important. They set the tone for the culture of the company. It is well known that "A" team members hire "A" employees, whereas "B" team members hire "B" or "C" employees. The initial team members also will become future leaders in the company, so having strong leadership skills is essential. One key realization is that in a startup, especially, you need to be flexible enough to handle multiple tasks—even tasks for which you have no prior experience. This means that in addition to a deep expertise in one area, team members need to be intrinsically smart, curious, and have a growth mindset. One way to determine the flexibility and willingness of potential hires to go beyond their area of expertise is to quiz them on topics related to their domain. For example, ask a product manager to mock up the UI for a specific feature, or ask a back-end developer how he or she would develop a specific front-end feature.

You should also look to hire doers across the board—even at the executive level. I have typically hired mid-level or director-level people initially instead of VPs (unless a really good candidate was available). At that level, these people not only have an execution mindset but also the strategic-level thinking capability to guide the overall direction of the company.

Build a Brand

Like any marketing campaign, you need to consider how to build a brand that will attract high-quality candidates to consider your company. A critical way to build a brand is to conduct high-quality PR for your company that gets people to get excited about the mission of the company. With Livemocha, for example, we got coverage in the local Seattle newspapers as well as the *New York Times* and the *Wall Street Journal*. This kind of coverage builds the trust and the credibility that you need to attract strong candidates.

Another way to be seen as a thought leader in the community is to sponsor startup or tech-related Meetup group meetings and give a talk about the technology you are building. Make sure that there are other people from your company to mingle with the audience so they can network and make more connections. You should also consider hosting talks on technical topics at your company and invite people at the Meetup groups to attend these talks at your company.

Referral Bonuses

Current employees are often the best source for leads on potential employees. The best way to incentivize your current employees to refer their former colleagues is to institute a generous referral bonus. After all, it will be a lot less expensive to pay your current employees than to pay an external recruiter who takes 25 percent of a hire's annual salary. You should make sure that all your employees know of any new job openings that you are posting. Keep hammering on these open positions every time you have a company meeting so people don't forget. You should also consider organizing an open house from time to time, so that the referred people can come in to chat with the founders and other employees.

Make it super easy to refer potential employees to your hiring manager. Once someone has been hired through a referral, send a note out to the company congratulating the employee who made the referral. Call out that person at the next company meeting as well.

Job Postings

Most job postings that I have seen are incredibly dull. You need to be creative and spice up the job posting to make it stand out compared to other openings that candidates will see. Describe how the candidate will be contributing to the overall strategy of the company and why that role is essential to the company's success. Describe the cutting-edge technologies that the person will be working on. Take the opportunity to also describe the culture of the company and how you have made your company a fun and rewarding place to work. Make sure your company website has a section specifically devoted to your culture and the values that you espouse.

Avoid the mistake of mentioning salary ranges in your job posting. If you make an offer at the low end or even the middle of the range, the candidate might feel insulted and will try to negotiate the salary to the high end of the range.

The following is an excellent example of a well-written job posting from Twitter. The job title itself is interesting enough to attract potential recruits and inspire them to read more about the job opportunity. The posting also does a great job of talking about the company and its mission in a way that is inspiring.

Tweeter in Chief

SAN FRANCISCO, NEW YORK OR ANY OFFICE IN THE US

A THREAD SORT OF:

- Tweet Tweet. You'll be @Twitter on Twitter. Our Tweeter in Chief. You'll set the tone of who we are and how we act, and talk to people on Twitter. No big deal.
- Twitter isn't like other brands. We're where all voices come together, where unique conversations happen every day. Twitter is what's happening in the world, and what people are talking about right now.
- We have our own distinct story to tell, but we're also host to the most amazing conversations in the world. We want to elevate and thank the people who use us. Spark conversations that highlight what unites us. Make the platform and world feel a little smaller.

- And yes, we want to tell the story of Twitter's purpose and product innovation. These things might be donuts, summoning circles, Serena Williams or the launch of Retweet with GIF.
- You are a master in the art of Twitter, and want to take that passion and expertise to the ultimate, metal level of @Twitter.
- You'll be writing the Tweets for @Twitter, setting the editorial direction and leading a team of incredible community managers. So every day you'll be reacting to culture, as it happens.
- You are extremely plugged into Twitter culture, stan culture, and culture in general.
- You are obsessed with building communities and how content travels on the platform. You know what it takes to have a strong social voice, and you practice what you preach.
- You are an expert storyteller and writer, and can apply that thinking to social voice, and creative activations in general.

REQUIREMENTS:
- You love Twitter, and are passionate about our purpose and story.
- Proven track record of leading the voice/social copywriting for influential brands, with a particular emphasis on Twitter. Show us Tweets!
- Razor-sharp editing skills; can digest the Twitter voice and apply to everything you do.
- Immersed in Twitter culture; you should know what's happening before we do!
- Understanding of the broader marketing landscape.
- A desire to work in a fast-paced, collaborative environment.

- Resourcefulness, attention to detail and comfort offering solutions and clarity where there is ambiguity.
- Proficiency crafting creative, inspiring stories that communicate complex concepts simply.
- FUN!

Interviewing Strategies

Most companies I know do a fairly haphazard job of interviewing job candidates. They don't do a good job of asking diverse questions or interviewing for cultural fit. I recommend that you come up with a variety of topics that you would like to interview the candidate about as well as the actual questions you will ask. Divide up the topics and questions among different people so that you have time to review all aspects of a candidate's background and experience. Make sure to ask questions to determine if they would be a good cultural fit as well as a good fit for a startup environment—in other words, taking initiative, dealing with ambiguity, work ethic, and so on.

Once an interview is done, make sure that each interviewer has provided written feedback. If you prefer, provide a simple template that people can fill out so you can capture feedback on all aspects of the interviewee's background. Ask each interviewer to provide a definite hire-or-no-hire recommendation. Finally, as a founder, make time to meet with each key potential hire and use some portion of your time to really sell the interviewee on the company (assuming that you think that the interviewee is a good hire).

Interview Follow-Up

It is very important to be professional and prompt with interview candidates after their interview with the company. If you are not going to make an offer, politely respond to the candidate that he or she was not a good fit for the company. Do not make the mistake of offering any specific reasons for why you declined to make an offer—it will only get you into trouble.

It is critical that you spend the necessary time and resources to conduct reference checks on potential employees. You shouldn't leave this task to your recruiter—instead, the hiring manager should be conducting the reference checks. You should ask candidates for references—managers, colleagues, and employees who have worked for them. You should also let them know that you will conduct blind reference checks as well—in other words, you will seek out other people they haven't named on their list of references (except for people at their current employer's). In doing the reference checks, you should figure out how to elicit critical feedback about the employee, as most references are reluctant to provide negative feedback. Ask them, for example, how they would rate the candidate compared to other people with whom they have worked. If the candidate is not in the top 25 percent, ask what attributes the person needs to have to make it to the top 25 percent. If you have a specific concern about the employee, mention the concern and ask if the reference agrees with your assessment and how you should manage the candidate so that the concern doesn't become an issue.

If you decide to move forward with an offer, do so promptly, as the candidate probably is considering other offers. Have the hiring manager or even a founder call the candidate to make the offer. If the candidate is going to be a senior employee, consider having your investor board member talk to him or her. Invite the candidate to come back to the company to address any further questions. Give the candidate no more than a week to make a decision on the offer and check in frequently to show that you are genuinely interested in getting him or her on board.

CREATING A VIBRANT COMPANY CULTURE

F ew startup founders spend time explicitly thinking about the culture that they want to establish at their company. They dive right into the problem of establishing product/market fit and generating revenues for their startup. Employees are hired because of how smart they are perceived to be, not how they might fit into the culture. As a result, the culture of the company can over time mirror the personality of the CEO, especially if the CEO has a strong and aggressive personality.

This was true when I worked at Microsoft. Like Bill Gates, we were all intensely competitive with a win-at-all-cost mentality. Many of Bill's key managers embodied Bill's personality with a penchant for rocking back and forth and yelling at employees if they had not thought through a problem. Microsoft's competitive culture had a big impact on the company's growth in the nineties as it became the center of the PC software universe. Ultimately, however, Microsoft's aggressive behavior caught up with the company in the form of the US Department of Justice's antitrust lawsuit. While Microsoft ultimately settled the case, it was a pyrrhic victory that was followed by more than a decade of decline as Microsoft missed many key innovations in the market.

Uber was another example of a company where the culture reflected CEO Travis Kalanick's win-at-all-cost bro culture. While Uber achieved tremendous success under Kalanick's leadership, it almost cost the company its user base when #DeleteUber became a popular hashtag because people were repelled by its toxic culture. A famous example is the story of Susan Fowler, an employee at Uber who suffered through sexual harassment at the hands of her manager. Even when Susan complained to human resources about her manager, that person was not fired by the company. Ultimately, the VCs behind the company and the board had enough of Travis Kalanick and forced him to resign as CEO.

Why Is Establishing a Company Culture Important?

A company culture models the behavior of the company and the decisions that it makes when the founders are not around. As a company grows, it is clearly not going to be possible for founders to be involved in every decision that the company makes. The company culture defines how employees interact with one another and with customers and how the company conducts its business. The company culture can have significant impact on employee satisfaction, customer satisfaction, and whether the company conducts business in an ethical and legal fashion. Oftentimes, a company culture can manifest in unpredictable ways when employees take the founder's behavior to the extreme.

Uber, for example, had a reputation for breaking rules as it entered different cities to establish its service. While one could argue that it had no option but to do so as cities were politically motivated to protect the taxi industry, they also undertook actions that one could argue were highly unethical. For example, in Portland, Uber deployed a secret feature in its app called Greyball. This feature would detect the local transportation officers from the Portland Bureau of Transportation who were looking to fine Uber drivers and not show any Uber rides around them. The Department of Justice is now reportedly investigating the use of this tool.

Creating a Long-Term Vision

The foundation of any company culture is the long-term vision for the company. It establishes the pole star that the company is shooting for and provides direction to the employees on the types of initiatives that it will invest in. Bill Gates's vision at Microsoft was "A computer on every desk and in every home." It meant that Microsoft would invest in software that went beyond simply making office workers more productive—it focused on making personal computers relevant, even essential, to every user at home. It was the key rationale that led my team at MSN.com to invest in search and the Hotmail acquisition to make the internet easy to use and accessible for consumers.

The long-term vision should be expansive and motivational for employees. Our vision with Livemocha was "To create lasting cultural connections and improve economic opportunities through language learning." A key feature of Livemocha was the ability to connect with native speakers throughout the world who could help develop your language proficiency. We felt that this was essential to develop strong language skills and also to create relationships that were essential in helping to bridge cultural boundaries and in helping users to gain a better understanding of disparate cultures. The other driving belief for Livemocha was that foreign language proficiency (especially English) was critical in accessing greater economic opportunities and lifting people out of poverty. I believe our vision with Livemocha was very powerful and even critical in our ability to attract an internationally diverse employee base that was motivated to make a difference in the lives of billions of people learning a foreign language.

Developing Your Culture's Value System

It is important that you start early with your cofounders to define the key values that embody the value system for your culture. The best way to do this is to have a brainstorming session where all the cofounders and key members of your management team sit down together to discuss the values that are important to each person. According to Molly Graham, a former manager for culture and branding at Facebook in its early days, founders should engage in an exercise in self-awareness and ask the following questions:[1]

- What are my strengths?
- What am I outstanding at?
- What sets me apart from the people around me?
- What do I value about the people around me?
- When I look at my friends, what are the characteristics they have in common?
- What qualities drive me crazy about people?

- How do I make my best decisions? (Think of a recent decision you made that had a good outcome. What process led to that?)
- What am I bad at?

You want to find the key commonalities from each individual list and identify no more than five key values that you want to get behind. Once you finalize your key values, make sure that you have been living up to those values as a founder from day one. I don't think it is realistic that you will suddenly start following certain cultural principles you have identified if they are not reflective of the founders' behavior. As they say, "A leopard never changes its spots."

I am a big fan of Amazon's Leadership Principles, which reflect the values that are core to Amazon. There are fourteen principles in total, which may be a lot for most people to remember. Of these, I believe the following five principles should be at the top of the consideration list for most startups:[2]

CUSTOMER OBSESSION
Leaders start with the customer and work back. They work vigorously to earn and keep customer trust. Although leaders pay attention to competitors, they obsess over customers.

OWNERSHIP
Leaders are owners. They think long term and don't sacrifice long-term value for short-term results. They act on behalf of the entire company, beyond just their own team. They never say "that's not my job."

LEARN AND BE CURIOUS
Leaders are never done learning and always seek to improve themselves. They are curious about new possibilities and act to explore them.

BIAS FOR ACTION

Speed matters in business. Many decisions and actions are reversible and do not need extensive study. We value calculated risk taking.

DELIVER RESULTS

Leaders focus on the key inputs for their business and deliver them with the right quality and in a timely fashion. Despite setbacks, they rise to the occasion and never settle.

Reinforcing Your Culture

A company culture can take a long time to establish. It is important for founders to live their values every day and set an example of employee behavior. They need to highlight good examples for employees at their company meetings. New employee orientation should be designed to focus on the key attributes of the company culture. Members of the management team should make time to provide their take on the employee culture at these orientations.

Icertis is a leading contract management company based out of Bellevue, Washington. The Icertis founders are big believers in the importance of culture. According to Samir Bodas, founder and CEO of Icertis: "One thing I didn't appreciate, that I appreciate more now, is how much culture matters. When I came out of business school, I thought culture was all BS. I thought it was all about making money, and as long as you put enough money in people's pockets, they will take the pain. That's absolutely wrong. To be able to articulate the culture through your values, and knowing how those values are used in action and how you live them—it makes a huge difference for people."[3]

The Icertis culture is captured in the following acronym—FORTE, which stands for fairness, openness, respect, teamwork, and execution. These attributes are the benchmark that the company uses when hiring people. The company also holds what it calls "FORTIFIED" sessions, which are four-hour-long sessions for forty people at a time to communicate and discuss their culture. At these sessions, participants discuss a number of scenarios that the company has actually faced. One scenario, for example, concerns an interviewee who receives strong reviews from interviewers. Later, however, interviewers learn that the candidate has a prior minor criminal record. Should the company hire this person despite the criminal record? This example typically brings up a lot of discussion around some of the attributes of their culture—for example, fairness and openness.

Another scenario is about an employee who is on a performance improvement plan (PIP). However, putting this person on a PIP did not result in any performance improvement by the end of the period. A decision is made to let the employee go. However, on the day that this person is to be informed, he tells the company that one of his parents has passed away. The person is still let go at that point. The case study discusses whether the company made the right decision or if the situation should have been handled differently. This example highlighted many of the cultural values important to the company—in other words, fairness, teamwork, and execution.

Operating in a Post-COVID World

The COVID-19 crisis forced companies to shut down their offices and make their employees work remotely from home. This was a big change for most employees, especially when, in addition, they had to manage young children who were also asked to stay home. However, the change has not been as disruptive as originally thought, and employees have generally felt that they have been equally productive working from home. They have also appreciated the extra time that they have gained from avoiding long and stressful commutes to their workplaces.

Given the positive experience with remote work, many companies—for example, Twitter—have changed their philosophy about allowing employees to work from home even after the end of the COVID-19 crisis. There are a number of benefits to doing so including the ability to be more competitive from a hiring perspective as well as being able to recruit from non-tech cities where employees may choose to relocate for a lower cost of living and a better lifestyle.

While working remotely has many benefits, there are also many downsides you need to consider as a startup founder.

REDUCED COLLABORATION AND CREATIVITY

While tools like Zoom have significantly alleviated the downsides of collaborating remotely, they haven't completely eliminated those downsides. It is just easier to have serendipitous meetings with coworkers to solve a pressing problem or brainstorm new ideas on a whiteboard when you are working together in an office. It is also a challenge to have meetings if some workers are working from an office and others are calling in remotely. The employees calling in remotely generally will have a harder time getting their voice heard compared to coworkers who are together physically in a meeting room.

REDUCED CAMARADERIE

Working long hours alone can be lonely. There is something to be said about working together in an office environment, engaging in idle chat in the break room, or going together to have lunch.

LEARNING AND DEVELOPMENT

In a lot of early-stage startups, there isn't a lot of written material to get someone up to speed on tools and processes. In an office environment, it is a lot easier to catch someone more experienced for a short conversation to answer any questions that might be blocking your work.

WORK HOURS

In an office environment, there's a lot of pressure to work late since everyone else is doing it. With a remote work environment, there's the risk that employees who are not self-motivated or don't have well-established objectives may goof off and not be as productive as employees working in an office.

I AM A BIG BELIEVER THAT, in the early stages of a startup, the founding team should work together in an office environment. If you feel that you need to work remotely, consider working together at least two hours a day in a coworking space or even sitting in a coffee shop. There are just too many issues that you need to discuss, whether it is a quick discussion or intense brainstorming on a whiteboard, and Zoom is just not as effective. However, over time, as the team grows bigger, it would be worthwhile to consider allowing team members to work from home on a permanent basis. It might even help you recruit employees you might not otherwise be able to attract. Once you allow employees to work remotely, then you need to adapt a number of strategies to make the remote workers operate effectively.

CREATING AN OKR-CENTRIC CULTURE

OKRs (objectives and key results) have become a popular methodology for setting goals and objectives and tracking progress against those goals. There are a number of SaaS-based OKR setting and tracking tools like Ally on the market that allow organizations large and small to manage OKRs throughout the company. For organizations with a large remote workforce where constant communication is a challenge, setting proper goals and objectives and tracking progress become even more important. A tool like Ally is also integrated with collaboration tools like Slack and Microsoft Teams so that users are frequently prompted to update their OKRs over Slack or Teams. As progress against objectives are updated through these tools, managers can interact with their employees and provide guidance to help them fully achieve their objectives.

ZOOM MEETINGS

If you are having meetings and any of the participants are remote, I recommend that the meeting be completely conducted over a tool like Zoom—in other words, each participant should be online, even if some employees are in the office. This way, the remote workers are not at a disadvantage compared to the workers in the office. If all the participants are working in the office, then it would be acceptable to have an in-person meeting. However, you have to be careful that people don't stop inviting the remote workers to their meetings so they can have in-person meetings.

RECONFIGURING THE OFFICE

If a significant number of employees are working remotely, then you don't need as much office space. You also don't need to have assigned seating. If some people come into the office, they can take up the desk space on a first-come, first-served basis. You can also consider leasing some coworking spaces so that remote workers can go to an office environment and interact with other people instead of working from home all the time. This will help alleviate the sense of isolation they might otherwise feel. Finally, since you will be spending less on office space, consider providing a onetime stipend to remote workers to allow them to set up their remote office properly—for example, invest in a standing desk, monitors, ergonomic chairs, and so on.

OVERCOMMUNICATION

Frequent one-on-ones and stand-up meetings over Zoom are essential to keep the communication going and to improve morale. Some companies have implemented the notion of "random" coffee meetings over Zoom to substitute for serendipitous meetings in the break room. Employees are paired up on a random basis for a short online meeting to discuss whatever is on their minds or even engage in idle chitchat.

Unlike in-person meetings where you can read the room and understand who is engaged and who is not, it is a lot harder to get everyone engaged in a Zoom meeting. It is much easier for shy or new employees to hide on Zoom and not provide their input on the issues being discussed. You should encourage the managers in your company to make sure that they track who is interacting on Zoom and who is not and to explicitly encourage the quieter members to contribute their point of view.

Proper documentation is key to ensuring that the essential processes are being communicated to new employees. A number of companies are using tools like Notion and Confluence to create company-wide wikis, document key processes, and provide status updates.

BECOMING
A GREAT LEADER

"Some are born great, some achieve greatness, and some have greatness thrust upon them." This quote from William Shakespeare in *Twelfth Night* is perfectly emblematic of the situation faced by most startup CEOs. I learned my managerial skills at Microsoft, but nothing really prepared me for the incredible leap that I had to make as a CEO for my first startup. I was lucky to have raised $15 million in funding during the height of the dot-com madness. However, within a few months, the market crashed and, even worse, I had to deal with the fact that our initial product had not achieved product/market fit. I had to navigate the company through a layoff and a product pivot and later consummate an acquisition by Research In Motion. Those were incredibly trying times, and I had to learn leadership skills on the fly to lead my team to a successful outcome.

Communicating Your Vision and Strategy

A key element of motivating your team to follow you through thick and thin is to clearly articulate your vision and strategy for the company and be able to defend it, especially when times get tough. You need to take every opportunity to communicate your vision and strategy, whether through company meetings or meetings to finalize the product feature set for the next release. At Livemocha, a key element of our strategy was to make our solution a crowdsourced platform that leveraged our 15-million-member global community to create language learning content. Our team really took this strategy to heart. Initially, Livemocha offered learning only in six languages through content that we had developed on our own. Our team built a crowdsourcing solution that allowed our community to translate our content into an additional twenty-four languages. We were amazed at how much work our community was willing to do for free and spoke to how Livemocha has won the hearts and minds of language learners all over the world.

Product-Centered but Multifaceted

A successful startup founder needs to be the person driving the overall product vision and strategy. The founder does not need to be a technical expert to drive product strategy, but does need to have a strong sense of the customer's pain points and needs to know the type of solution required to address those needs. Even when you hire a vice president of product, you need to be deeply involved in customer discussions so you are always on top of understanding the customer's needs in order to effectively direct the product strategy.

A successful leader needs to be multifaceted as well as have an in-depth understanding of all aspects of the company's business. In addition to the product strategy, the leader needs to be driving the overall business model for the company. Without a sound business model, your company will not generate the revenue growth needed to attract venture capital investment. Finally, the founder needs to be the best "sales" person in the company to sell the company's vision and strategy. It's not necessary to get into the weeds of how to effectively run a sales organization. However, the sales team needs to have the confidence that, if they bring the CEO into a sale, the CEO can help them close the deal.

Hiring and Firing Effectively

Hiring, at least in the initial stages of the company, is one of the most critical tasks that a CEO needs to take on. The people that you hire will eventually hire other people in the company, which sets the tone for the company's culture and competence. To convince potential employees to take a significant pay cut and join an unproven startup takes an enormous amount of persuasion skills. In all my startups, I successfully hired strong candidates while convincing them to take a 15 to 20 percent pay cut. It helped that I had a successful track record that I could point out to people. However, a key part of the sales strategy is to outline the vision for the company and get people excited about the opportunity to come in at the ground floor to build a great company. Even when I was not the primary decision maker, I was the "as appropriate" whose role it was to sell the vision for the company.

Firing people who are not a good fit for the company is an equally important skill. People who are not carrying their load or are a bad cultural fit should be let go quickly so they don't start demotivating other high-performing employees in the company. I once had a member of the management team who I felt was not a good fit with the company culture. Unfortunately, we were in the middle of an acquisition discussion for the company. I was, however, concerned about letting that person go in the middle of an acquisition discussion as I thought it might affect the deal. In the end, we decided not to take the acquisition offer, and I let the individual go at that point. In hindsight, I waited too long to take action. I should have acted sooner even if it meant some disruption to the acquisition discussions. The risk to the company cohesiveness and morale was much greater and harder to repair.

Keeping Your Company Afloat

Keeping your company financially viable at all times is one of the greatest challenges that startup CEOs face, especially in the early days when there aren't many proof points to convince investors. I was lucky to have raised funding for my two startups when times were really good. However, I also immediately encountered significant downturns after raising funding that I had to manage my way through. I have also raised funding at the depths of the global financial crisis. There are four key elements to keep your company solvent:

- **Execute, execute, execute:** Great execution is everything. In the early days of your startup, you need to achieve product/market fit. You need to develop your business model and show that you can get customers to pay you enough money to build a venture scale business. Finally, you need to develop a sales engine to get to $1 million

ARR so you can raise your Series A funding. Thereafter, you need to achieve strong growth in revenues so you have a line of sight to $100 million in revenues in five to seven years after raising a Series A. If you demonstrate an ability to grow revenues in this manner, you will always be able to raise funding even in the worst of times.

- **Be good at raising funding:** You have to be great at telling a compelling story to potential investors to convince them to fund your company. You have to convey enthusiasm at all times and be prepared to pitch a lot of investors and take rejections. The key, of course, to raising funding is to show traction—whether it is end user/customer engagement or early signs of revenues. If things are going really well, be prepared to raise more money than you need, even if it means additional dilution, because you never know when the next market crash is going to happen.

- **Manage your burn:** During the dot-com boom, most companies went crazy hiring hundreds of employees and spending money on expensive furniture and parties before proving that they had a viable business model. No wonder when the dot-com bust happened most of these companies went under. In contrast, I managed to keep my burn rate low with all my companies, which allowed me to stay alive longer until I could engineer an exit for my company. Of course, you also have to make the necessary investments to drive your business forward. You can't build a great business just by keeping the burn really low.

- **Act quickly during a crisis:** There's always a good chance that you could encounter a major market crash while you are working on your startup. Even if you have raised a significant amount of money, you should move quickly to cut your expenses so you can make your funding last for a much longer time. I discuss the actions that you need to take in chapter 27, "Managing in Downturns."

MANAGING YOUR
BOARD OF DIRECTORS

Managing your relationship with your board of directors is an essential task for a startup CEO. The first order of business should be to ensure that you build a strong board that can provide oversight and advice for your business. Since the VCs get to select who represents their interests on the board, it is important that you select your investors carefully. You should conduct as much due diligence on your investors as they conduct on you. Don't just conduct due diligence on the firm—rather focus your inquiry on the specific partners who will be joining your board. Try to understand how strong they are in terms of providing strategic and operational advice, whether they tend to be hands on or do they leave it to the CEO to run the company, how supportive they are when the company is going through a downturn, and if they have fired a founder CEO in the past and under what circumstances.

In order to manage your relationship with your board, it is first important to understand what role the board has in managing the company.

Hiring and Firing the CEO

One of the key responsibilities of a board is to replace the founder CEO if the board feels that he or she is not up to the task. Alternatively, you might have a technical founder who is not interested in being a CEO and would prefer to play the CTO role. Generally, the board will hire a recruiting firm to help recruit a new CEO in addition to leveraging their own contacts. It is important in this situation for the founders to be as heavily involved in interviewing and vetting the CEO as the VC board members. The board should ideally look for candidates who have either been successful entrepreneurs themselves or have served as executives at successful startups. Generally, successful executives at large companies don't transition well to smaller startups where they typically don't have the resources to execute their plans as they would at a larger company.

Look for candidates who have a long list of accomplishments and have been successful in trying circumstances. Another key attribute of successful CEOs is whether they have been successful in recruiting people who have worked for them in the past. This implies that they have strong management skills and will similarly be successful in recruiting their past employees to your startup.

Pay attention to any red flags that come up in the interview. A startup that I am familiar with hired a CEO even though there were red flags that the person was quite arrogant in the interviews and came across as a know-it-all. As CEO at a previous startup, however, this person had significantly accelerated revenue. One of the VCs on the board did a background check and got positive reviews that led to the hiring of this person as the CEO. However, this CEO turned out to be a failure as he rapidly increased the burn and hired incompetent executives. The company finally had to be sold at a significant discount to its last round valuation. It turned out that the VC had not, in fact, done enough due diligence on this person. "Due diligence" means going beyond the references that the person provides to get a strong and accurate perspective of the traits and the skills that the person brings to the job.

Once a CEO has been hired, it is important that the board leaves it up to the CEO to run the company. If the board includes experienced operators, it can sometimes be tempting for these board members to interfere in the company operations. This could happen because the company is not performing well, or the board members feel that the CEO is not up to the task. If that is the case, then it is important for the board to conduct a formal review of the CEO and his or her plan and interview other executives and employees of the company to determine if the CEO is doing a good job. If it turns out that the CEO is not doing a good job, then a decision should be made quickly to fire the CEO and hire a replacement. If you are on the receiving end of interference from a board member, seek advice from other board members on how to handle the situation. Ask for a meeting with the offending board member and articulate your concerns to see if you can negotiate mutually acceptable rules of engagement. If necessary, spend more time with the board member to address any concerns prior to a board meeting.

Approval of the Strategic Plan and Budget

While board members should not involve themselves in the day-to-day running of the company, it is important that they approve the strategic plan and budget for the company. The strategic plan should cover the product strategy, go-to-market plan, potential partnerships, revenue plan, expenses, key hires, and any fundraising needs. Once the plan has been approved, the board should review progress on a monthly basis. On a quarterly basis, the management team should present any changes to the plan, in particular to the operating budget, and get direction and approval from the board. The board should also have an extended discussion of the company's strategy and fundraising needs to determine if any changes in the plan are required.

Management and Employee Compensation

The funding documentation will typically provide for a compensation committee to determine the management compensation. The recommendation of the compensation committee is then voted on by the entire board. VCs generally have access to compensation reports that help them determine the appropriate compensation to give to management team members.

The board also approves the option grants to the management team and employees, but is not involved in individual employee decisions. It only approves the overall head count and total expenses. Before granting options to management and employees, the CEO should come up with the overall budget for utilizing the option pool until the next round of funding. The board should then approve the option pool budget. At every board meeting, the CEO should list the option grant for employees hired recently and get board approval for the recommended option grants. The CEO should identify which option grants exceed the approved recommended grant for that position.

As mentioned earlier, following a financing round and every year thereafter, the CEO has to commission a 409A valuation study of the price of the common stock. The board then has to approve the common share price recommended by the valuation study. This price is then the strike price for option grants that are issued for a one-year period following the study. If there's a financing event prior to the end of the one-year, safe-harbor period, the 409A valuation needs to be performed again as there will be a new valuation for the company.

Partnerships, Fundraising, and M&A

A key area that most boards don't pay enough attention to are potential partners and acquirers. In my last company, Zoomingo, our board used to require us to keep such a list and update the board on any changes at every board meeting. If you have a good sense for potential acquirers in your space, it is often a good idea to explore partnerships. You never know when these discussions will lead to an acquisition interest. This is what happened with my first company, TeamOn, which was acquired by Research In Motion (RIM). Initially, the discussions started with the intent of creating a partnership in which we would license our technology to RIM. RIM was interested in pursuing the consumer market and wanted to license our technology so BlackBerry users could access a range of proprietary consumer email services like Hotmail, AOL, CompuServe, and others. TeamOn was the only email solution that had done the hard work to reverse engineer these email services. Ultimately, RIM decided that this technology was too strategic for them and that it was important to acquire TeamOn rather than merely license this technology.

Boards play a key role in fundraising. The VCs on your board will be instrumental in connecting you to other VC firms that can invest in your company. The board will also assist you in determining how much funding you should raise and what valuation you should target for your fundraising. The VCs can also back-channel the reaction from the VC firms that you have met. This will help you better hone your pitch to subsequent firms.

Finally, the board has a critical role in any M&A (mergers and acquisitions) discussions. It is the responsibility of the CEO to bring any M&A interest to the attention of the board (even if it doesn't want to sell the company) as the board has a fiduciary responsibility to maximize the interests of the shareholders. If there's serious interest, it is typically advisable for the board to hire an investment bank to solicit other potential bidders for the company, thus maximizing the acquisition price. The investment bank will also help the board decide what is a fair valuation for the company. Finally, it will help the company negotiate the best price.

Structuring Your Board Meetings

I have come across very few entrepreneurs who actually look forward to board meetings. It is often treated as a "chore" and a source of stress that consumes a lot of cycles that would otherwise have been used more productively to move the company forward. However, if you have a strong board, the board meetings can be a valuable exercise allowing you to think deeply about your business and get feedback from smart and experienced board members on key strategic issues facing the company. Board meetings also force the management team to prepare a well-thought-through update that they can also utilize to update their employees and keep them focused on the company's priorities and strategy.

Generally, most CEOs structure their board meetings as simply status update meetings. Typically, very little time is devoted to discussing substantive issues that the company is facing. Similarly, there is often no specific ask where the CEO seeks help from the board—for example, an introduction to a potential business partner or help with hiring a specific member of the management team. I would, therefore, suggest a format where roughly half the time is spent on a status update and an equal amount of time is spent discussing the top two or three strategic issues. Ideally, you should spend three to four hours to hold your board meetings so that there's sufficient time to provide a proper update and hold a good discussion on the key issues.

Your First Board Meeting

There are two important topics that need to be discussed in your first board meeting. First, you need to get all your board members on the same page with respect to your company's strategy, competitive positioning, and business model. The content of the presentation should be essentially the same information that you presented in your investor pitch. While your investors will have seen the presentation before, it is a good idea to go over it again so you can flesh out any issues that they may have with your plan.

The second part of the presentation should be a discussion of your goals and objectives for the year, a detailed go-to-market plan, and your planned budget for the fiscal year. You should make sure that the board has approved both your budget and hiring plan for the next year in your first board meeting.

Standardizing Your Board Presentation

Following the first board meeting, you should create a standard presentation format that is consistent across different board meetings.

This way it becomes much easier for the board to track progress across multiple board meetings. The Sequoia Capital board deck[1] format is a good format to use for your board deck.

You should make it a point to send your deck to the board at least forty-eight hours in advance so that the board members have enough time to review the deck and prepare for the meeting. This way you can also spend less time on the status update and more time discussing the key issues that you face.

Communicating with Your Board

I highly recommend calling your board members a week in advance of each board meeting. You should give them a heads-up on any performance issues—for example, if you missed your revenue objective for the month, any high-profile deals you lost, or loss of any key team member. This way there are no unpleasant surprises at the board meeting. You should also give them a heads-up on the key issues that you would like to discuss at the board meeting so that they have time to think about the issues and formulate an opinion.

Logistics

I highly recommend that the board meetings be conducted in person. It becomes very difficult to have a substantive discussion if some of the board members are calling in. Board meetings should be conducted monthly, especially in the early days when there is rapid progress and it is important to get frequent feedback from the board. I also recommend that most board meetings be followed by an evening dinner. This allows the board to build a good working relationship with the company executives.

Communicating with Your Team

Finally, I highly recommend that the CEO leverage the board presentation to give essentially the same presentation to the company. This is a good way to keep everyone up to speed on the company's progress and share the board's feedback. If possible, ask one of your board members to join the company presentation from time to time so that employees can hear the board's perspective. Of course, you can remove any confidential matters from the company presentation such as acquisition interest and financing-related matters.

Board meetings don't have to be a chore if they are structured properly. Once the presentation format is set, it shouldn't take more than half a day to create your board presentation. You will find that your board members and employees are a lot more aligned with the company's mission, and you can expect to receive valuable feedback and help from the board to move your company forward.

DEVELOPING
A BUSINESS MODEL

D eveloping a robust business model is one of the most
important tasks that you can perform for your company. A
business model defines how you will acquire customers and
what your customers or third parties will pay for your product or
service. If you are a B2C (business to consumer) offering, you will
likely rely on SEO, SEM, and web/mobile advertising to drive traffic
to your site and sign up customers. If you are a B2B (business to
business) offering, your sales strategy will depend on whether you
are targeting small businesses or large enterprises. If you are
targeting small businesses, you will likely rely on SEO, SEM, and
web/mobile advertising to attract customers. Your website will need
to be designed for self-service so that customers can purchase your
offering on their own without requiring a salesperson. If, on the

other hand, you are targeting large enterprise customers, you will use SEO, SEM, and web/mobile advertising to drive traffic to your site, educate the customer, and capture leads. Thereafter, you will need to utilize a sales force to call on customers to arrange for online or in-person demos. Sales cycles will also stretch to several months as your sales organization convinces all the stakeholders to choose your product.

There are a number of business models that you can pursue depending on your offering. Here's a list of some of the most common business models employed by tech-oriented products and services.

Advertising

Advertising is a fairly standard business model for B2C applications, and it is easy to incorporate advertising into your application by leveraging existing ad networks. According to the IAB (Internet Advertising Bureau) report, internet advertising equaled $124.6 billion in 2019. Revenues increased by 15.9 percent over 2018. Mobile internet advertising revenues increased 24 percent from $69.9 billion in 2018 to $86.7 billion in 2019, making up almost 70 percent of total internet advertising. On a worldwide basis, digital advertising was expected to grow by 18 percent to $333 billion. Globally, Google, Facebook, and Alibaba capture most of the ad spend.

While advertising can be fairly easily implemented, it will impact your overall user experience. It is also not likely to generate significant revenues for you unless you have hundreds of millions of monthly active users with a highly desirable audience for which you can charge a high CPM (cost per mille). To maximize your advertising revenues, it is important that you are able to provide demographic, interest-based, or location-based targeting and allow advertisers to bid for your inventory as you can with sites like Facebook. It might be a good idea, in addition, to consider a premium offering for your application that provides additional features and removes the advertising. A good example is Spotify, which allows its paid users to download songs to mobile devices while also removing any advertising in between songs.

Affiliate Marketing

Affiliate marketing is another revenue-generating strategy to consider for B2C application developers. By 2022, affiliate marketing is forecast to generate more than $8 billion in revenues, making it considerably smaller than internet advertising. Generally, affiliate marketing should be considered when the content on your site is aligned with the items that you are promoting via affiliate marketing. As a result, the affiliate promotion or ads can be more organically integrated into the content of a B2C application. For example, if you are a social networking site for book reviews, you can incorporate affiliate links to books on Amazon and get an affiliate marketing fee every time someone clicks through on a link and purchases a book. Another example is Trip Advisor, which generates fees from hotels when users click through on hotels listed on its site.

Affiliate fees can be of three types:

- Pay per sale—this is the most common model and is typically utilized by e-commerce companies that pay you every time someone completes a purchase after clicking through on your link
- Pay per click—this is similar to the Google CPC model where you get paid every time someone clicks through on your affiliate link

- Pay per lead—this model is typically utilized by enterprise companies who pay you a fee every time they capture a lead coming through your link

E-commerce Model

E-commerce sales have grown tremendously over the last twenty years. US e-commerce sales exceeded $600 billion in 2019, constituting almost 16 percent of all retail sales. Global e-commerce sales reached $3.5 trillion in 2019. With the coronavirus pandemic, e-commerce penetration has accelerated dramatically as shoppers avoided going into retail stores. In the United States, Amazon has become the dominant player with almost a 50 percent share of the US e-commerce market. As a result, many e-commerce companies are setting up shop on Amazon as well as hosting their own website using solutions like Shopify. Third-party sales now make up almost 58 percent of Amazon's total sales. E-commerce companies can expect to pay between 8 and 25 percent selling commission to Amazon for selling through its platform. In addition, sellers can expect pick, pack, and ship and inventory storage fees when they utilize Fulfillment by Amazon services.

In the last decade, we have seen the emergence of e-commerce-only brands like Warby Parker, Allbirds, and Stitch Fix. These startups have had to spend an enormous amount of money to establish their brands, which they have successfully done with the help of venture capital funding. Some, like Stitch Fix, have implemented interesting subscription-based pricing models while implementing AI-based technology to deliver customized clothing targeted to their customers' tastes. A number of startups like The RealReal, OfferUp, and Poshmark have also emerged in the used-goods space and achieved multibillion-dollar valuations.

Freemium Model

Freemium offerings have become quite common for B2C applications and increasingly so for many B2B applications. The common approach is to offer a somewhat feature-limited version of your application that is typically ad supported. The user is then offered an upgrade to a paid version that offers additional features with no advertising. With Spotify, for example, the premium version offers unlimited skips, offline audio, and high-quality audio in addition to no advertising. Spotify has had tremendous success converting free users to paid users. More than 45 percent of its monthly active users are paid users. Typically, a good conversion rate is between 5 and 10 percent.

Another way to structure a freemium offering is to offer a capacity-constrained version of your application for free and require users to pay for additional capacity. Capacity could be defined as storage or megapixels for photos (in the case of Google Photos). Dropbox, for example, offers a free version that comes with two gigabytes of storage. However, if you want additional storage, then you have to start paying for the application. Dropbox also offers enterprise plans for business users and teams that incorporate additional security features in addition to a significant amount of storage.

A final strategy you can employ is to offer a time-limited free version. Apple Music, for example, offers a free three-month trial, after which you have to pay. The key challenge is to figure out the duration of the free offering. If it is too short, you may not be giving users enough time to try out the service and get hooked to it. If it is too long, you are leaving money on the table. To figure out the appropriate amount of time, start with a longer period and then watch how customers engage with your application. For example, you might start with a one-month free trial. If it turns out that the customers who end up paying for the offering are generally fully engaged after two weeks, then consider shortening to a two-week trial. Take into account what kind of trial period your competitors are offering as you will likely have to match that period.

A freemium strategy is increasingly being pursued by end-user-focused enterprise applications. Slack is a prime example that offers a free version. The free offering is constrained by total amount of storage (five gigabytes) and access to ten thousand of the team's most recent messages. This is a very clever strategy, as teams can easily exceed the five-gigabyte limit and accumulate more than ten thousand messages over time. Slack is successful in converting more than 30 percent of its users into paid users, which is a remarkable number.

SaaS (Software as a Service) Model

Most enterprise applications are now increasingly offered with a SaaS model. Microsoft Office is a great example of an application that changed its model successfully from a traditional product licensing model to a SaaS model. A SaaS model generates less revenue initially compared to a traditional software licensing model, but over time can generate substantial revenues, especially when the churn is low. The conversion to a SaaS model is one of the key reasons Microsoft's revenues have been so robust over the last five years. They have successfully converted a majority of their enterprise and consumer customers to a SaaS model.

Generally, most companies offer tiered pricing where the customer pays more per user as the size and the complexity of the business grows. Typically, the terminology that companies use is Standard, Advanced or Plus, and Enterprise. Typically, the Advanced or Plus tier will offer features such as app integrations, single sign-in, unlimited storage, and 24/7 customer support. The Enterprise tier requires that users contact the company to negotiate a contract and typically offers advanced administration, archiving tools, integration with enterprise mobility management, and designated account management and customer success teams. Slack's example of tiered pricing is shown in Figure 4.

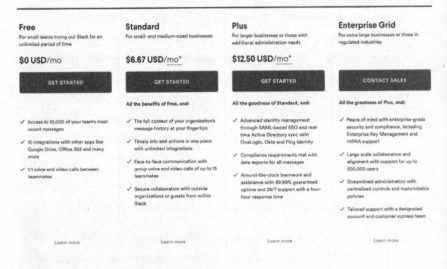

Figure 4. Slack's Tiered Pricing

Usage-Based Pricing

Usage-based pricing models are typically offered by infrastructure providers like Amazon Web Services (AWS) and Twilio, which offer computer services, storage, telephony services, and so on. Customers pay a monthly fee based on actual usage of the services. For example, Twilio charges $0.0075 to send or receive a message. Typically, these services will offer volume discounts, and after a certain point you can directly negotiate a price with the service provider. To drive predictable revenues in this model, you can offer a prepayment option where customers can prepurchase a certain quantity of the offering at a discount. For example, AWS offers "Reserved Instances," allowing the prepurchase of a certain amount of computer or storage instances for a year at a significant discount.

Transaction Fees

This model is typically utilized by payment and e-commerce companies. For example, Stripe charges 2.9 percent + $0.30 for each successful transaction (see Figure 5). Companies like Shopify and Kickstarter also have a per transaction fee. Shopify, in addition, also has a SaaS model for hosting your e-commerce site.

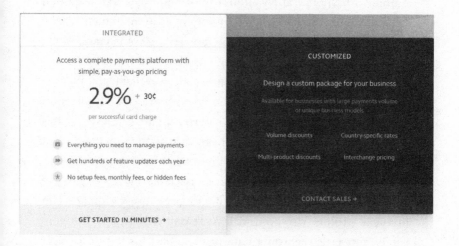

Figure 5. Stripe Pricing

Lead Generation Model

Collecting leads and selling them to enterprises is a common strategy in the academic and enterprise space. In the academic space, there are companies like All Star Directories that provide resources for students interested in vocational training and degree programs. They collect information about the students and sell the leads to providers of these vocational programs. Similarly, in the enterprise space, there are a number of sites that provide resources for companies looking to purchase specific types of enterprise solutions.

These sites provide reviews of these enterprise solutions and will collect information on interested companies and sell these leads to providers of these enterprise solutions.

Selling Data

A number of mobile applications capture user data that they then sell in an anonymized fashion to other applications and enterprise customers. A prime example is the mobile app Foursquare, which captures user location data through its Foursquare and Swarm applications. It makes this location information available to other applications and retailers through a Foursquare API (application programming interface). Retailers, for example, can leverage this data to check to see if their advertising is leading to increased foot traffic to their stores. Mint is another example of an app that collects data about the users' financial transactions and sells aggregate data to financial institutions looking to target users with a certain financial profile. However, with increased regulations and consumer concerns regarding data privacy, startups should be very careful about selling data to third parties.

UNDERSTANDING UNIT ECONOMICS

One of the key mental models that VCs use to understand the profitability and the long-term viability of startups is to understand the unit economics of the business. Most startups are unprofitable for years on end, but if they have strong unit economics that are trending in the right direction, then VCs will continue to fund them. There are essentially two key metrics that startups need to track—customer lifetime value (LTV) and customer acquisition cost (CAC). Generally, VCs like to see an LTV to CAC ratio that is at least 3:1. This allows the business to generate enough margin to cover its operating costs and generate a profit for its shareholders.

Customer Lifetime Value (LTV)

The customer lifetime value measures the profitability of the customer over the lifetime of the customer's relationship with the company. Imagine that you are an e-commerce site and you conduct an SEM campaign to attract customers to your site. Let's say you attract a hundred customers who make total purchases of $5,000 each for a gross margin of $1,500. You register these users, then a month later email them with a new promotion, and another fifty of them make purchases totaling $2,500 for a gross margin of $750. None of these customers make any subsequent purchases for the foreseeable future. The LTV for these customers will equal the total gross margin of purchases/total number of customers. In this case, the LTV for each customer will be equal to ($1500 + $750)/100 = $22.50.

As another example, let's say that you have a SaaS subscription offering that's priced at $10/month with a 60 percent gross margin and a monthly customer churn rate of 2 percent. The LTV for the subscription offering will be calculated as follows:

LTV = Monthly Gross Margin/Monthly Churn Rate

In this case, the LTV will be equal to $6/2 percent, which equals $300. This means that you can spend up to $100 to acquire the customer to maintain at least a 3:1 ratio of LTV to CAC.

Many people make the mistake of using the revenues they earn to calculate the LTV, which is not correct. Figure out the gross margin for your offering and use that in calculating your LTV.

Customer Acquisition Cost (CAC)

The customer acquisition cost measures the cost of acquiring each customer who makes a purchase. Going back to the e-commerce example, let's say that you spent $1,000 on the SEM campaign to acquire a hundred customers—your CAC would equal $10. Since you received only $22.50 as the LTV, you didn't hit the minimum threshold of a 3:1 ratio of LTV to CAC. As a result, you need to either find a less expensive acquisition channel or do more marketing to your acquired customers to get them to purchase more and, therefore, increase the total LTV.

As another example, let's say that you have an enterprise sales force of five salespeople calling on customers. Each salesperson closes an average of ten customers a year. You pay each salesperson $200,000 per year in salary and commissions. In addition, you spend a total of $100,000 on a marketing campaign to generate leads that the salespeople can call on. Your average CAC = ($200,000 + $100,000/5)/10, which equals $22,000. To maintain an LTV to CAC ratio of 3:1, you should make sure that your LTV is at least $66,000 per customer.

You should also understand your LTV and CAC by customer segment. If you have a solution that is purchased by enterprises of different sizes, you may find that the LTV and CAC for a small-business customer may be very different compared to a large-enterprise customer with a long sales cycle. Your pricing strategy, as a result, should be to charge a significantly higher price for large-enterprise customers to take into account the higher customer acquisition cost. In turn, to justify the higher price, you will need to offer differentiated features that large-enterprise customers value as compared to small-business customers.

Note that in calculating the CAC, you should only include customers acquired through paid acquisition channels and not customers you acquire organically. It is certainly possible that some of the organic customers come because of advertising that they see from you. To be conservative in calculating your CAC, include only the customers who click through on your advertising and become customers. If you like, you can also calculate a "blended" CAC that takes into account your organic customers with the assumption that many of them were influenced by your marketing campaigns.

LTV and CAC can also change over time. As you offer more compelling features that improve engagement, you will find that the churn rate will come down, which in turn will increase the LTV. You will also find that CAC will typically rise over time as you acquire more customers until it stabilizes in a narrow range. Advertising costs, for example, will increase as you spend more money to acquire customers. Zulily, an e-commerce startup, found eager customers in its infancy at a relatively inexpensive CAC. However, as it expanded beyond its early customers, it found that its CAC and churn rates increased significantly, which resulted in the sale of the company.

PROTECTING YOUR INTELLECTUAL PROPERTY

I n this chapter, I will cover patents (but not trademarks and copyright), which is the main intellectual property concern for most startups. A patent is a legal right to keep other parties from making, using, or selling the claimed invention for a limited time. A patent does not confer a legal right for you to make, use, or sell the claimed invention. Patents can be fairly time consuming and expensive to file, especially for startups that have limited time and funding. It is worthwhile filing a patent application if the invention is core to your business model and offers a critical competitive advantage. Software patents these days are also quite difficult to obtain, given the current case law.

Patents cover new and useful ideas (inventions). To be patentable, the inventions they cover must be useful, novel, and nonobvious to

Design Patent (Bottle Shape)

Trademark

Trade Secret (Formula)

Coke Bottle (Intellectual Property Components)

one with ordinary skill in the art. Inventors typically file patent applications in the country where they reside—for example, the United States Patent and Trademark Office for American inventors. Patents generally last for twenty years from their filing date. Filing a patent application gives you the right to mark your invention as "Patent Pending."

The first step in patentability analysis is to determine if a prior patent has been granted for your claim or has been previously disclosed by you or others. This way you can save a significant amount of money if there is prior art related to your invention. Even if there is prior related art, your patent attorney can do a much better job of accentuating the differences for your invention in your patent application. You can conduct a patent search on your own using Google Patents, which is a powerful patent search engine. If you can afford it, a better strategy is to hire a specialized patent search firm. It will generally take two to three weeks to conduct the search, and it will cost you anywhere from $2,000 to $3,000.

Patents: The Provisional Application

Once you have decided to protect your invention with a patent, the next step in the patent application process is to file a provisional application. This way you can avoid the significant legal fees for filing a patent application immediately. Note that in the United States, you have one year from public disclosure of an invention to file a patent application. However, internationally, you lose the right to apply for a patent the moment you disclose your invention.

It is relatively inexpensive to file a provisional application. The attorney time is generally $3,000 to $5,000.[1] The patent office filing fee is about $280 versus more than $1,000 for a large entity. Note that there is no such thing as a "provisional patent," only a provisional patent application. It provides a filing date for a non-provisional patent application. It also allows you to mark your invention as "Patent Pending." The provisional application can be refiled after one year, but you can't keep the original date. This is a good strategy for early-stage startups that have enough funding to pay for a provisional patent application but not for the full patent application, which they can defer until they raise their Series A funding.

The cost of filing for a non-provisional patent is around $10,000 to $15,000, including patent office fees. The patent office fees can be half that for small entities, which are companies with less than five hundred employees. There are also prosecution costs for filed applications. It is generally impossible to predict the number of back and forth interactions with an examiner. It is usually two to five interactions—expect at least two. Each response generally costs between $2,000 and $3,000. You don't want a "first action allowance," which means that your patent has been accepted immediately, since it indicates that the scope of your patent was probably too limited. The cost of an issued patent is around $1,000.

Post-issuance of a patent, you will incur significant maintenance fees, which are as follows:

- $1,600 after 3.5 years
- $3,600 after 7.5 years
- $7,400 after 11.5 years

If the patent is no longer adding value, consider not paying the maintenance fee, at which point the patent will expire. Expired patents can be revived, but it is an expensive process and not guaranteed.

Foreign Patents

Foreign patents are generally outside the scope of most startups until they have raised tens of millions of dollars, since they are typically quite expensive to file. There are two types of patent applications: direct filings and PCT (Patent Cooperation Treaty) applications. With direct filings, you file directly in each country where you want patent protection. The PCT application is also known as an International Patent application. This strategy should be used only if you want to file in a large number of countries. It is generally more expensive to file, but the costs can be spread over a larger period. It can be thought of as an "option contract" to hold open the right to file in several countries later.

Foreign patents are expensive. You should plan on budgeting $20,000 per country. About one-third is due up front, one-third over three to five years to set grant, and a final one-third to maintain. Many countries require annual maintenance fees to keep the application pending.

MANAGING
IN DOWNTURNS

As a serial entrepreneur, I have had the misfortune of going through two major downturns—first, the dot-com crash in the late nineties, and then the global financial crisis–related crash in 2008. We have now had a major market crash almost every decade for the last three decades, including the coronavirus-induced economic crisis of 2020. These downturns are extremely hard to predict, and it's virtually impossible to prepare in advance of these downturns. Typically, the markets have generally done extremely well before each crash, and the crashes happened with surprising speed with the markets dropping 30 percent or more in a matter of a few weeks. These downturns can also last for several years, making it even more challenging for startups to cope with the situation and survive the downturn.

These recessions are typically characterized by massive layoffs as companies look to conserve cash when their revenues take a significant hit. Consumer demand is also similarly affected. Startups, in particular, are highly vulnerable because they have limited funding, and their revenues take a hit when companies and consumers cut back on nonessential spending. Raising funding becomes extremely challenging as VCs slow down their pace of new investments and focus on existing companies. Valuations also take a significant haircut when valuations of comparable public companies are also affected.

When these downturns happen, it is extremely important that you move with urgency and put together a plan that can get you through the market crash in one piece. Make sure to get advice from your board members, who likely have been through these situations in the past and can help guide you through the crisis. However, it doesn't have to be all doom and gloom. Remember that many great companies, including Facebook and LinkedIn, emerged during the depths of the dot-com crash and thrived despite the challenging circumstances in which they were born.

Assess and Secure Your Revenues

Your first order of business is to determine if your revenue is affected and if there has been any impact to your customer acquisition metrics. For example, is your trial-to-paid conversion ratio going down? This may take some time to determine as customers may not immediately back off from purchasing your product. Contact your existing customers immediately to see if any of them are planning on canceling your service or contract. Consider offering your customers special incentives to stay on with your offering if any customers seem inclined to cancel. Once you have a better picture of how revenues are being affected, you should develop an updated revenue plan to present to your board and get their feedback. The updated revenue plan will help you determine to what extent you will need to reduce your expenses to keep your burn rate at the same level.

Reduce Expenses

It is very likely that your revenues will be significantly affected by a market crash. The impact is often greater for startups since most companies and consumers will likely view new offerings as nonessential. You will need to, therefore, cut your expenses at least proportionate to the loss of revenues that you are experiencing. The other factor to consider is that you will need to make your existing funding last much longer as raising funding will be very challenging. If you were planning on raising funding in the next twelve months, plan for eighteen months. As a result, you will have to cut back even more so you can last longer. Once you have figured out your revenue picture and the duration of time you need to make your funding last, update your operating plan and get feedback and approval from the board.

Employee Layoffs

Unfortunately, employees typically make up a large portion of the cost structure of a startup. If your revenues have been significantly impacted, it will be hard to avoid a layoff, which can be very difficult for most startup founders. However heartless this might sound, you need to move quickly on this front or you could be hemorrhaging valuable cash every month that you wait to take action. You should also plan appropriately in terms of how many people to lay off. Founders are typically reluctant to lay off people, and they will initially make a small cut and then later realize that they have to make more cuts, resulting in rolling layoffs over an extended period. This can be extremely demoralizing for employees who will be left wondering if they are next. You should, therefore, make the hard decision to make one deep cut and stick to that plan as long as possible.

Another option is to initiate pay cuts across the company. Pay cuts may not buy you much unless you have a significant number of employees. You run the risk that your top performers will leave, which they can do even in bad times. If you do consider a pay cut, consider it mainly for the founders and the management team because it will be largely symbolic. It will send a message that you and your management team are willing to make necessary sacrifices for the good of the company. The percentage of the pay cut could vary across founders, management team, and employees. Founders, for example, could stop taking a salary if they can afford it or take a 50 percent pay cut. The management team could take a 25 percent pay cut, and employees could take a 15 percent pay cut. Try to limit the duration of the pay cut. If the economy turns back up again, you could reinstitute the original pay that management and employees had received prior to the market crash. If you are able to raise another round of funding, consider giving bonuses to your top employees to make up for their lost salary. (However, don't word it as such as other employees may feel entitled and get upset.)

In March 2000, when the dot-com bubble burst, we faced a similar challenge. Fortunately, I had raised $15 million in funding for my company TeamOn and was fairly frugal in hiring people, especially compared to other dot-com companies that had hired hundreds of employees. My board gave me very clear direction to cut back on our head count, and we had to go through a very painful reduction of employees from around sixty to twenty-five employees. I announced to the company that I would stop taking any salary to demonstrate to my employees that I was more than willing to make necessary sacrifices to ensure the survival of our company. As a result of these steps, we made our funding last well into 2002, when we were finally acquired by Research In Motion (BlackBerry).

Employee layoffs are never easy and should be handled with great care and dignity. You should consider doing the layoff on a Friday. This will give the remaining employees enough time to process the news and come back with a fresh perspective the following Monday. Take the time to talk to the remaining employees on that Monday to remind them about the vision and mission of the company. Talk about the operating plan that you have reviewed with the board to turn things around. Utilize weekly company meetings to discuss the progress you are making and rebuild the confidence of the team.

In conducting the layoff, you should have each manager personally talk to all affected employees and tell them how sorry they are to take this action. Ideally, make sure that there's a human resources person involved in each conversation. Keep the conversation short and to the point. If you are providing employees with a severance package, have them sign a severance agreement indemnifying the company. Give them at least two weeks of severance, which is the least you can do under the circumstances. If you can afford it, give employees who have been with the company longer a more generous severance—for example, an additional week of severance for each year served. Give the employees enough time to collect their belongings and say goodbye to their colleagues. Finally, contact other CEOs and recruiters you know and send them résumés of your employees in case other companies are hiring.

Airbnb is a great example of a company that effectively handled a very painful layoff of 25 percent of its employees in the midst of the COVID-19 crisis. The company offered generous benefits to its employees who were laid off:

- Fourteen weeks of base pay with an additional week for every year served
- Dropped the one-year cliff for vesting equity
- Twelve months of healthcare coverage through COBRA
- Job search assistance through an alumni talent directory and placement team

Secure Venture Debt for Your Company

During any major crisis, venture capital financing will seize up for an extended period. And those VCs still investing will only do so at a significantly lower valuation. In these situations, it would be prudent to look at venture debt as a way to extend the runway for the company and allow the company to raise funding when the markets have recovered. Of course, even the venture debt lenders will be cautious about whom they lend to, and you will only be able to raise funding from them if you can demonstrate that you still have a sound business model (despite taking a hit on sales). The backing of your VCs is also critical to securing venture debt funding. I have twice been able to raise venture debt, during the dot-com bust and the global financial crises, and can vouch for the flexibility that this funding provided to me in extending my runway.

Renegotiate Vendor Contracts

You should look at any significant long-term commitments to see if you can reduce them. At TeamOn, for example, we had a real estate lease for a larger space than we needed, especially once we had significantly cut back on our staff. I went to my landlord and convinced him to cut back on the space that we had committed to. Fortunately, the landlord was eminently reasonable, which helped significantly reduce our monthly outlay on rent. At the end of the day, it turned out well for the landlord because the company expanded its space significantly after my company's acquisition by RIM.

Be Flexible with Customers

Just as you need vendors to be flexible with you, you need to be flexible with your customers. If your customers can't afford to pay you all that they have committed to, postpone the payments until later. You will create lasting customer relationships as a result. During the financial crisis, one bank, for example, converted all its loan payments to interest-only payments for a period in order to lessen the monthly payments that its customers had to make. In another example, Zoom made its offering free for schools during the coronavirus crisis. Also, take a closer look at customers who may have special needs that you can better satisfy. For example, Icertis, a contract management company, heard early on that their customers were looking to their contracts to understand and address the commercial implications of the coronavirus crisis. The company deployed a swat team to help customers with this data analysis.

Be Transparent with Employees

Any major crisis will create significant concern among your employees. They may be afraid that the company will go under or that they will lose their jobs. It is very important, therefore, that you take action quickly and communicate a clear plan to your employees. Don't shade the truth—your employees will see through any spin and will stop trusting you. If you are up front with your employees about the challenges that you face, you will find that they will step up and go the extra distance to help the company succeed. Remind them about the mission of the company and why it's an exciting mission that they can rally behind. Communicate often, highlight the progress you are making, and celebrate even small successes. Point out where certain employees have gone beyond the call of duty to secure a deal or help their customers.

PART V

FINDING AN EXIT

SELLING
YOUR COMPANY

M ost entrepreneurs dream that one day their company will
have a successful, multibillion-dollar initial public offering
(IPO). However, of the companies that do have a successful
exit, most find it by selling the company. According to a report by
Crunchbase, the average successful startup has raised $41 million
in venture capital and exited for $242.9 million since 2007.[1] Among
those that were acquired, Crunchbase reports startups raised an
average of $29.4 million and sold for $155.5 million. Those
companies that exited via IPO raised $162 million before going
public and raised an average of $467.9 million through IPOs.[2]

This chapter will discuss how to create interest in your company from potential suitors, how to select an investment banker to

manage the sale of your company, and how to successfully negotiate a great price for your startup.

The TeamOn Acquisition

In 2001, after our small business–hosted email solution failed to get significant traction, we decided to pivot to building a mobile email solution for commodity handsets, which had started to offer internet connectivity. Prior to making the pivot, we did a lot of great work to reverse engineer a number of proprietary email systems at that time such as Hotmail, AOL, CompuServe, Microsoft Exchange, and Lotus Notes so that our small-business customers could access their existing email while transitioning to our email solution. This technology formed the basis of our mobile email solutions where anyone with a WAP browser (wireless application protocol browser—yes, that's what the web browsers on the phone were called in those days) could access their email account. It took us a good six months, but we secured the interest of T-Mobile to offer our solution on their GPRS handsets.

In the meantime, we started approaching other handset manufacturers to see if they would be interested in licensing our solution. Our idea was unique compared to other mobile email solutions, which only allowed you to access a standard POP3 or IMAP4 email account. However, most popular email systems were proprietary in nature, and TeamOn was the only solution that could offer access to all the major proprietary email systems. One of the handset manufacturers we approached was RIM, the makers of BlackBerry. RIM at that time had a relatively small installed base but was starting to gain popularity among investment bankers, VCs, and corporate executives. However, they only provided access to corporate email accounts on Microsoft Exchange or Lotus Notes.

In the 2001–2002 time frame, RIM started working with wireless carriers around the world to offer its BlackBerry solution on its data networks, allowing it to significantly increase its reach. While these wireless carriers had a large number of enterprise customers, they had a much larger number of prosumer users who needed access to their proprietary email account. They communicated this requirement to RIM so that it could start offering the BlackBerry solution to these users. Fortunately, for RIM, we had exactly the solution that they needed to satisfy the wireless carriers' needs.

Initially, our discussion with RIM started off as a licensing arrangement. However, as they started to think through their strategy for the long term, which was to pursue the larger prosumer/consumer market, they realized that our technology was simply too strategic for them not to own it. They decided that it would be much better to acquire our company as opposed to license our solution. This way they could also keep the technology out of the hands of their competitors, including Microsoft, Palm, Handspring, and others.

In the early spring of 2002, RIM informed us that it was interested in acquiring TeamOn. We were thrilled to hear the news because RIM was the leading wireless email solution of the time, and it had relationships with all the major US and European wireless carriers. While we had started to get traction with the T-Mobile relationship, the market situation following the dot-com crash was still grim. We had survived by being prudent with the $15 million in funding that we had raised in 2000. We did have a term sheet for follow-up funding from one of our investors; however, it was at a significantly lower valuation than our previous round. If we were acquired by RIM, we would be able to get our technology in the hands of millions of wireless consumers around the world. As a result, we decided to engage with RIM to discuss the acquisition.

Once we had interest from RIM for an acquisition, we decided to engage an investment banker to see if we could solicit interest from other companies to get more bidders to the table. Unfortunately, no other companies came to the table with acquisition interest (the M&A market had essentially frozen following the dot-com crash), so we were forced to negotiate only with RIM. The initial offer from RIM was lower than we expected and disappointing to everyone. We decided to seek a higher offer from RIM and suggested a meeting with the RIM CEOs (yes, they had a CEO, Jim Balsillie, and a co-CEO, Mike Lazaridis).

The meeting went well, and RIM came back with a higher offer, which we decided to accept. TeamOn employees also received stock options in RIM, which did very well as the stock took off in the next five years. It took some time for RIM to integrate the TeamOn technology, but once we both did the work, the result was called Black-Berry Internet Service email, which serviced more than 50 million BlackBerry users at its peak until BlackBerry's demise at the hands of Apple and Google.

Planning for an Acquisition

While most entrepreneurs would love to go all the way and achieve a multibillion-dollar IPO, the reality is that most startups find an exit through an acquisition if they are lucky. The key, as they say, is for your company to "get bought, not sold." The best time to sell your company is when the economy is booming and your company is experiencing strong growth year over year. Typically, in these situations, acquisition interest is strong and revenue multiples are high. However, many entrepreneurs can get cocky about the prospects for their company, thinking that the economy and company growth will continue to be robust in the foreseeable future. Inevitably, the economy weakens or the company's growth slows down, making it a bad time to sell the company. If an entrepreneur is hesitant to sell in strong economic times, one strategy to consider is to sell to a private equity firm and sell a majority stake in the company. This way, the entrepreneur can gain significant liquidity but also retain enough stake to benefit from the future upside if the economy continues to be strong.

Sometimes, the issue is that the founders are too eager to sell when an acquisition offer comes along but the VCs think that it would be better to hold off for a future IPO. To avoid this conflict, it can be beneficial for the VCs to allow the founders to take some money off the table by liquidating some portion of their shares. This can be done by allowing the founders to sell some portion of their founder stock in a subsequent financing where future investors purchase these shares as part of their investment in the company. By gaining some liquidity, the founders can be more rational about considering acquisition interest in the company.

If your company is looking for an exit, you should strongly consider hiring an investment bank to help you sell the company. They have relationships with potential acquirers in your industry that might be a good fit, and they can help you put together an effective pitch for the company. The involvement of an investment bank will also signal to potential buyers that you will have a well-defined process and multiple interested parties at the table. This is likely to get you a higher sale price that you might not be able to otherwise achieve on your own.

Another strategy to getting bought as opposed to being sold is to build relationships with potential acquirers well before an acquisition. You should build a list of these potential acquirers and share that with your board members—they may point out others that you haven't thought of. From this list, identify those that are not directly competitive and could potentially distribute your solution. Reach out to these companies to see if you can negotiate a distribution relationship or a partnership to get promoted on their platform. Seek meetings with the CEOs of these companies to make sure that you get visibility on their radar screen. It may take a year or more for these companies to reach the conclusion that they should acquire you, but in the meantime you will have shown them that your solution is getting good traction in the market.

If you do get an acquisition interest from another company, you need to inform your board members and have a strategic discussion with them about whether pursuing acquisition makes sense because it can be highly distracting and time consuming. You have to be careful that you don't get pushed into pursuing acquisition by your VCs, who may not understand what impact it will have on your time. Any significant acquisition discussion could easily take up a third of your time.

A good example of a VC mismatch was the situation that we faced with Livemocha a year and half after our Series A investment. We received acquisition interest from an established language-learning company. Since Livemocha was growing very rapidly, our VC firm had an unrealistic expectation that the company was worth more than $100 million despite the fact that we had little to show in terms of monetization (we were very early with our monetization experiments at that time). The board decided that we should pursue the acquisition interest and instructed me to hire an investment bank even when it seemed fairly clear that the potential acquirer would not pay anywhere close to the VC firm's expectations. I ended up spending three months of valuable time in the acquisition discussions. We ended up with a good offer that would have provided the investors a return of two-and-a-half times their investment, but the VC firm rejected the offer as it was well below their expectations for the company.

Another factor to consider is if your startup is generating significant network effects in a large winner-take-all market. In that situation, there may not be *any* price at which you will want to sell your company. Facebook, for example, had an offer to sell the company at a $1 billion valuation to Yahoo. While this would have been a significant payday for Mark Zuckerberg, it would have been a huge mistake for him to sell the company. Conversely, it is very likely that the Instagram founders are kicking themselves for selling their company to Facebook for a billion dollars. Today, Instagram has more than a billion users and is worth far more than the price at which it was sold.

Hiring an Investment Bank

If you have an acquisition offer or you are considering the sale of your company, it is generally a good idea to hire an investment bank to help shop your company and get the best sale price. It can help identify potential acquirers and get multiple parties to the table by leveraging its existing relationships with leading companies in your space. It can also help in determining the appropriate valuation range for your company as well as help negotiate the sale.

You should seek your board's advice in identifying the appropriate investment banks to interview to help you sell your company. Ask other startup CEOs who have gone through an M&A process. In selecting your bank, look for banks that have strong expertise in your industry sector. Make sure that they typically manage sales in the valuation range appropriate for your company so you can get the attention that your company deserves. Ask them who would be appropriate buyers for your company and what kind of contacts they have at these companies. Check references to make sure that their previous clients have been happy with the work they have done for them and that they have the industry contacts they claim to have.

Most investment banks will charge a monthly retainer fee as well as a success fee that is a percentage of the sale of the company. The success fee can range from 2 to 4 percent depending on the sale price. Typically, the fee will be higher if the investment bank gets you a higher sale price. There is also a minimum fee regardless of the sale price for the company, which, of course, you pay only if the company has been sold. Retainers can range from $10,000 per month to a onetime fee of $50,000 or even $100,000 if it is expected to be a multi-hundred-million-dollar sale. The banks will ask for a twelve- to eighteen-month exclusive on the sale of the company so the bank gets the success fee even if they were only peripherally involved in the sale to the final acquirer. Note that these terms are all negotiable, and you should rely on your board and law firm to help you negotiate an agreement with the investment bank.

Once the investment bank has been hired, it will spend four to six weeks preparing a confidential information memorandum (CIM) about your company with your help. The CIM will provide information about your company, product offering, competitive positioning, and your business model. The bank will work with you to develop a list of potential acquirers that it will contact to get the process going. In addition, separately, it will work on valuation comps and develop a valuation range that it will share with you and your board so you know what sale price is reasonable for your company.

Once the CIM has been prepared, the investment bank will initiate the marketing phase of the sale process. They will contact each of the target companies and provide them with a teaser document, including a nondisclosure agreement (NDA) to sign if they are interested in getting more information. Once an interested party has signed the NDA, it will be provided with the CIM and presentations will be set up with the management team. Once the presentations have been given, the investment bank will issue a process letter to the interested parties asking about their interest, valuation range, and the time frame in which they would be able to pursue the acquisition. This will typically help narrow down the list to serious buyers. At this point the investment bank will work with the CEO and the board to determine who are the top two or three companies the bank wants to seriously negotiate a deal with.

The investment bank will then ask the final candidates to provide their best offer to the company. Once these have been received, the bank will have a discussion with the CEO and the board to determine the best offer and how to maximize that offer. This is where the investment bank will truly earn its keep.

Typically, there are several aspects of the offer that the CEO and the board have to consider. Many acquisition offers contain an earnout that can be a significant component of the acquisition price. The other aspect is the management compensation. The management is offered incentives to stay beyond the acquisition and to achieve certain performance milestones related to the earnout. In addition to compensation offered by the purchaser, the selling company's board may also institute a management bonus that is tied to the sale price that is finally achieved.

Once a buyer and an acquisition price have been determined, a letter of intent (LOI) is signed with the acquiring company. It normally takes forty-five to sixty days to complete the acquisition. The acquiring company will conduct full due diligence of the company to validate the information that was provided to it. Finally, the lawyers will draft the acquisition documents to consummate the acquisition.

Managing Company-Wide Communications

Acquisitions can be highly distracting to employees within a company. You should keep information about a potential acquisition as confidential as you can for as long as possible. You will, of course, have to let the management team know of any acquisition interest since they will need to be involved in some of the discussions and preparation. To keep things confidential, you should even keep your acquisition-related board meetings off-site. Otherwise, employees will ask why you are having an unscheduled board meeting.

Once the acquisition enters the due diligence phase, it becomes much more difficult to keep things confidential as the potential acquirer will likely need to talk to finance, key developers, and operations. At that time, it would make sense to organize a company-wide meeting to inform everyone of the pending acquisition. Be prepared to tell employees about what will happen to their stock options, if their options will have any value from the sale, and if they will be able to keep their jobs post the acquisition. You will also have to discuss what the acquiring company's plans are with your technology if that has been communicated to you.

Negotiating an Acquisition

Successfully negotiating a good acquisition price for your company will depend on a variety of factors. As mentioned earlier, ideally you will consider putting your company up for sale when times are good and not when the economy or your company's growth has stalled. Another key strategy is to get multiple bidders to the table for the acquisition. This is why it is important for you to hire an investment bank as it is much more capable of shopping your company to a wide swath of potential acquirers. The investment banker can create a disciplined process to herd all the interested parties on a tight timeline to make sure that potential acquirers don't draw things out. The bank can also play off various players against each other to extract the best sale price for the company.

Another factor in driving up a high price is to understand how your technology fits into the acquiring company's strategy and how critical it is to their growth. When I was at Microsoft, I led the acquisition of Hotmail, which we ended up acquiring for roughly $400 million. At that time, Hotmail only had 10 million users and revenues of around $2 million. However, at MSN, we viewed email as a core addictive application that we had to provide to our users.

MSN.com at that time was late to the game and had a lot of work to do to catch up with industry-leading web portals such as Yahoo, Excite, and others. We needed to grow rapidly to catch up to the other players, and Hotmail offered a key customer acquisition engine as it was growing rapidly. Even though we paid a very high price for Hotmail, it turned out to be a good acquisition for Microsoft as Hotmail grew over time to more than 300 million users.

While you need to understand the technology fit with an acquiring company, you should also understand which group within the company stands to gain the most from the acquisition. You should make sure to develop a strong relationship with the head of that group as the group will be critical to driving a successful acquisition of the company. With the Hotmail acquisition, I made sure that my vice president and group vice president at MSN were brought into the deal and were strong advocates, especially given the high price. The Microsoft Exchange email group was opposed to the acquisition as they thought that they could quickly develop a competing solution to Hotmail. However, we felt very strongly it would take too long for Microsoft to develop a competitive solution and that we would lose valuable time in the market. In fact, at one point, Bill Gates sent out an email to all the group vice presidents at the company saying that he was moving forward with the Hotmail acquisition and that if anyone wanted to object they should do so soon. When I learned of the email, I literally ran to my group vice president's office and convinced him to draft an immediate email supporting the acquisition. I knew that, otherwise, we would run the risk that someone would come out against the acquisition, and it would turn the tide of the momentum that we had built.

A final factor that will determine your acquisition price is whether your company is being bought or sold. If your company is being bought and you have a strong financial position—in other words, strong year-over-year growth and strong cash position—then you have an opportunity to negotiate a strong premium over the current market valuation of your company. Your investment banker should be able to provide all the necessary market comps to justify the valuation that you feel the company deserves. The key to get a high premium over the market valuation is to act as if you are not really interested in selling the company. In the Hotmail case, for example, while the founders were interested in selling the company, the VCs backing the company were not interested in selling. The market at that time was at the height of the dot-com bubble and the VCs felt that they could do a billion-dollar IPO for the company. As a result, Microsoft had to pay a very high acquisition price as it knew that the company had a credible alternative to go public at a very high valuation.

GOING PUBLIC

Taking a company public is a dream for most startup founders. However, only as companies get closer to doing an IPO do they realize what a significant decision it is. An IPO provides many benefits, including providing liquidity for founders, VCs, and employees. However, companies face significantly greater scrutiny and relentless expectations from investors. Any earnings missed can be devastating for most companies as the stock price gets hammered, creating significant turmoil and employees. The process for getting ready for an IPO is a long one requiring a minimum of six months of preparation as well as the incorporation of proper financial controls and governance that can be very time consuming and expensive. And once the IPO is successfully executed, the work is not done as the company gets on a faster and faster treadmill to meet investor expectations. As a result, the average tenure of a company staying private has increased from 6.5 years to more than 10.5 years from founding. This has also been caused by the availability of late-stage funding from entities like SoftBank.

Pros and Cons of an IPO

There are many benefits to going public. These include:

- Provide liquidity for the founders, investors, and employees
- Raise significant additional funding to grow the operations of your company
- Gain the currency needed to make acquisitions
- Attract and retain talented employees
- Enhance the reputation of the company
- Attract a wider customer base and marquee customers—for example, F1000 customers
- Diversify the investor base

There are also significant implications of doing an IPO.

- Significant IPO expenses. The underwriters will charge 6 to 7 percent of the proceeds. In addition, there are fees related to legal and accounting advisors and printing costs. There are also other fees such as the SEC filing fee, the exchange listing fee, and any Blue Sky filing fees.
- Significant public expenses. Going public requires quarterly and annual filings, annual reports, and proxy materials. To ensure proper financial reporting and

compliance, you will need to hire a significant finance team to handle the new responsibilities. You will also incur significant public relations costs and auditor's fees for attestation of internal controls.

- Loss of privacy. You will now need to disclose a significant amount of information that will be valuable to competitors. This includes extensive financial information and compensation and security holdings of corporate executives.

- Increased scrutiny and performance pressure. Once a company goes public, it is under constant pressure to meet short-term performance metrics that make it difficult to invest in the long term. If a company fails to meet analyst expectations, the penalty on the stock can be quite significant. There's also significant risk that the company will lose analyst coverage if it continues to disappoint investors.

- Potential for shareholder activism. If the company falters in its financial performance, there's significant risk for shareholder activism. This can be very distracting for the company management, and it creates the risk that the company is forced to take short-term actions to boost the stock price at the expense of long-term investments. It can also create the risk that the company has to bring on new board members who represent dissatisfied shareholders.

- Vulnerability to hostile takeovers. Since the company is public, any other company can make a tender offer for all its shares, making the company vulnerable to a hostile takeover. The board also has a fiduciary responsibility to consider all legitimate offers that are beneficial to shareholders.

- Restrictions on insider sales. Insiders are generally restricted from selling their shares at the time of the IPO and for six months thereafter. Even after that, insiders and corporate executives don't have the luxury to sell their shares at any time lest they be accused of insider trading.

- Litigation risk. Given the increased disclosure requirements and the passage of the Sarbanes-Oxley Act of 2002, which protects investors from fraudulent financial reporting by companies, there are increased opportunities for class action lawsuits targeting the board and the management. The cost of litigating these lawsuits can be significant.

Are You Ready to Go Public?

Before a company goes public, it should conduct a thorough analysis of its readiness to do an IPO. There are several factors that the company should evaluate.

REVENUE GROWTH AT SCALE

To go public, a company should have at least $100 million in revenues (though there have been companies like Zillow that have gone public with far less) and a growth rate exceeding 30 percent a year (for two prior years and an expectation for two years into the future). It means that the company has achieved a certain level of scale in its market and is able to both retain customers and grow its customer base. Growth is most directly correlated to valuation as compared to other metrics such as margin. Ideally, investors should have line of sight to a billion dollars in revenue, which suggests a significant market potential and that the company is a leader in its category.

PREDICTABILITY OF REVENUES

There is nothing that investment analysts hate more than to see a company miss its forecast, which makes them look bad to their clients. In fact, they would like the company to beat its forecast and raise its forecast for subsequent quarters. Predictability of revenues suggests an experienced management team that has strong control and visibility on all aspects of its business. It also suggests a business that has a strong competitive position as it grows above market rates compared to traditional competitors in its business.

PROFITABILITY

Most technology startups that go public are not profitable, and most analysts don't expect them to be profitable very soon. However, the market does like to see a path to profitability for the company in the following six to eight quarters. This is why companies like Uber and Lyft have had disappointing IPOs since the competitive dynamics of the business make it very hard to predict when, if at all, these companies will attain profitability. Lack of visibility regarding profitability suggests weak unit economics as well as a weak competitive position where acquiring customers is very expensive and the companies don't have the market power to raise prices.

COMPETITIVE POSITION

It is not the number of competitors that concerns investors; it is how strong a competitive position the company has in the market. Does it have superior technology compared to the other players in the industry that can sustain themselves over time? For example, Snowflake, Inc., has built its data warehousing product from the ground up for a cloud native environment. As more companies migrate to the cloud, Snowflake has become the de facto choice compared to other vendors whose technology was not built for the cloud. Similarly, the market likes companies that have significant network effects. Airbnb, for example, has strong network effects and not surprisingly had a strong public debut as no companies have emerged that can go head to head against it.

LEADERSHIP

The quality of the leadership team, in particular the CEO and the CFO, is critical to a successful IPO. While the CEO may not have prior experience taking a company public, it is helpful to have a CFO who has done so successfully. It is not surprising, therefore, to see companies hire a CFO who has a strong reputation on Wall Street a year or two prior to going public. It is also helpful for the company to have hired independent board members who have been on the boards of public companies. If the management team has not run a public company, it is a smart idea for the CEO and CFO to engage potential investors in conversations well ahead of the IPO. This allows the investors to develop a sense of comfort in the management team and develop a belief that the management team knows what they are doing.

FINANCIAL OPERATIONS AND CONTROLS

The Sarbanes-Oxley Act of 2002 significantly raised the bar for financial reporting for public companies. The JOBS (Jumpstart Our Business Startups) Act of 2012 provides time relief for certain areas of financial reporting for emerging growth companies (EGCs). However, the amount of time and preparation for a company to get ready for the public reporting requirements upon going IPO can take a year or longer. Public companies also need to file on a quarterly and annual basis once they have gone public based on the SEC's strict accounting and disclosure guidelines for reporting. It is, therefore, essential for companies to have the discipline and capability to start reporting internally on a quarterly basis so they know that they have the organizational muscle do so properly once they go public.

Are You an Emerging Growth Company (EGC)?

The JOBS Act of 2012 was designed to ease the on-ramp for smaller companies to do an IPO. This was followed by the FAST (Fixing America's Surface Transportation) Act of 2015, which had some further provisions to make the process easier for EGCs. EGCs are broadly defined as companies that meet the following criteria:

- Less than $1.07 billion in gross revenue
- Less than $1 billion in issues of nonconvertible debt in a three-year period
- Not a "large accelerated filer," as defined in Exchange Act Rule 12b-2. A large accelerated filer is a company whose aggregate worldwide market value of the company's voting and nonvoting common equity held by nonaffiliates (or public float) is $700 million or more.

According to the SEC, EGCs are permitted as follows:

- To include less extensive narrative disclosure than required of other reporting companies, particularly in the description of executive compensation
- To provide audited financial statements for two fiscal years, in contrast to other reporting companies, which must provide audited financial statements for three fiscal years
- Not to provide an auditor attestation of internal control over financial reporting under Sarbanes-Oxley Act Section 404(b)

Most startups that plan to go public will fall in the EGC definition and can, therefore, take advantage of the less onerous reporting requirements.

Preparing for an IPO

The IPO preparation can be a long, lengthy, and complex process. There are a number of tasks that companies have to complete in order to get ready for an IPO.

HIRE A CFO

You need to hire a well-regarded CFO well before an IPO. Ideally, the CFO has prior experience taking a company public so is not learning the process on the job. Besides understanding how to take a company public, the CFO needs to have a good handle on the business model and the underlying risks of meeting growth and profitability expectations. The CFO also needs time to build out the finance function and hire a well-regarded auditing firm before the IPO. The finance function needs to be ready to close the books and report on a quarterly basis as it would once the company goes public. You want to avoid any kind of restatement of results as it will be devastating for the credibility of the company.

REBUILD THE BOARD

Investors will often look at the quality of the board in addition to the CEO/CFO team in making their investment decision. Ideally, you want to have board members who have significant public company governance experience. In addition, the SEC and stock exchanges have guidelines about having independent board members on the board. In the early stages of a company's life cycle, most of the board members represent investors who may not have public company governance experience. As a result, you will have to consider replacing these board members as you get ready to go public. You also want to give the new board members enough time to become familiar with the business and help you in navigating the IPO process.

HIRE THE LEAD UNDERWRITER

The process of hiring a lead underwriter should happen a year or two before a company goes public. Ideally, you are talking to these firms while you are conducting your late-stage financing. There are a number of factors that you need to consider in selecting your lead underwriter. The reputation of the lead underwriter is critical to the success of an IPO. The highest-ranked underwriters will have more experience leading IPOs. Institutional investors will likely pay more attention to an IPO that is led by a reputable underwriting firm. The reputation of the underwriter will also affect the quality of the syndicate that they are able to organize to gain wide distribution for your shares. A key factor in determining the capabilities of the firm is to understand the nature of their distribution relationships—do they have relationships primarily with institutional investors and do they have strong retail distribution as well? You also want to ask for the calendar of their IPO offerings to make sure that you will get enough attention from the underwriting team as you prepare to go public. Finally, you should understand the reputation of the research analyst that will be reporting on the company and how well respected he or she is in the market.

READINESS ASSESSMENT

The company needs to complete a readiness assessment that involves a detailed evaluation of all aspects of a company's key functions. Here are some the areas that you need to evaluate:

- Evaluation of your auditor's independence.
  Sarbanes-Oxley prohibits a company's auditors from providing certain affiliated services such as legal and valuation services.
- Auditing of financial reports. A company that goes public must have audited statements and interim (reviewed) financial reports.

- Finance team readiness. The finance team needs to be able to publicly report on a quarterly and annual basis in a timely manner. It needs to have controlled and accurate close processes in place with no post-close rework and adjustments.

- Prepare for Sarbanes-Oxley compliance. The Sarbanes-Oxley Act contains eleven major sections with responsibilities for management, board, and auditors around finance, accounting, and corporate governance. The sooner that a company has the controls in place, the better off it is. There are also requirements for the board. A majority of the board members have to be from outside the company. The board must also have an independent audit committee.

- Review of executive compensation. Once a company goes public, the compensation of the top executives must be disclosed. Accordingly, the board should review the compensation so that the company is not unduly criticized by institutional investors.

BUILD AN IPO TEAM

The company will need to assemble a top-notch team of experts that can guide preparations for successfully executing an IPO. The key members of the team include the following:

- A securities counsel that is well versed in securities laws.
- A lead investment banker/underwriter that has successfully taken companies public. The lead underwriter works with the company to develop the registration statement, coordinates the roadshow, puts together a syndicate of investment banks, and underwrites the IPO. The underwriter's agreement with the company usually comes in one of two forms—a firm

commitment where the investment bank agrees to purchase all of the company's offerings, or "best efforts" where the bank only commits to doing its best to market the offering.

- A capital markets advisor who provides independent advice to companies throughout the IPO process. This advisor helps in selecting the investment banks to manage the IPO process and negotiate the structure and the fees, as well as help craft the investment story, the marketing strategy, and the pricing and timing.
- An independent auditor that has experience in public financial reporting as well as experience with IPOs.
- A financial printer responsible for printing the registration statement and prospectuses with rapid turnaround.

Preparing the Registration Statement

Preparing the registration statement can be a complex undertaking involving the management team, underwriter, accounting firm, and legal counsel. The company's management team should take an active role in drafting the registration statement and not rely just on the underwriter and legal counsel as they know the business the best.

Here are the different parts of a registration statement:

- **Prospectus summary:** This is a short summary describing the company, its business, the type of securities being offered, the amount of estimated proceeds, the intended use of the proceeds, and principal risk factors. Since this is the first section, it should be crafted carefully to properly communicate the "story" behind the company and get investors excited about investing in the company.

- **Risks:** This is typically a long laundry list of risks that the company faces in successfully executing on its business. This section typically lists risks related to technology trends, competition, potential legislation, the company's dependence on a few major customers, and so on. It is wise to list every conceivable major risk as otherwise the company faces litigation risk for not adequately discussing a potential risk.

- **Use of proceeds:** The company should discuss the planned use of the IPO proceeds. This is important to do correctly as the SEC requires the company to report on the actual use of the proceeds after the IPO. The use of proceeds can range from debt reduction, acquisitions, R&D expenses, marketing expenses, and so on.

- **Dividend policy:** The company's dividend policy should be outlined though it is not unusual for an emerging growth company not to issue dividends.

- **Capitalization:** The company should present the capitalization of the company both pre- and post-IPO.

- **Dilution:** When there is substantial disparity between the effective IPO price, the book value, and the price that was paid for existing shares owned by officers, directors, and major shareholders, the resulting dilution of the purchaser's equity interest is shown here.

- **Information about the company's business:** The company must provide extensive information about its business. This includes information about the company's products, services and markets, competition, industry trends, market opportunity, business plan, and so on.

- **Financial information:** The company needs to present audited balance sheets, an income statement, a cash flow statement, and changes in shareholder's equity. Interim

financial statements are required if the fiscal year-end
financial statements are more than 134 days old.

- **Information on company's officers, directors, and
  principal shareholders:** The company needs to describe
  the business experience of its executive officers and
  directors; the security holdings of directors and principal
  shareholders; and transactions with and indebtedness of
  officers, directors, and principal shareholders.
- **Executive compensation:** The company needs to provide
  information about the compensation of the executive
  officers of the company including salary, bonus, stock
  awards, option awards, pensions, and amounts payable
  upon termination
- **Management discussion and analysis:** In this section, the
  management provides a discussion of the company's
  financial condition and results of operation. It should be
  written as objectively as possible and should mention
  both favorable and unfavorable developments.

Managing the IPO Process

The first step in the IPO process is to reach an understanding with
the lead underwriter. Once this is done, the company enters a quiet
period where it has to be careful about engaging in aggressive promotional activities. One exception is for EGCs—they are allowed to
engage with potential investors to gauge their interest in the offering. The company then engages in parallel activities to get ready for
the IPO. These include preparing the registration statement, preparing materials for the IPO roadshow, and undergoing the due
diligence required by the underwriter.

CREATE A WORKING GROUP

The company needs to pull together a working group that consists of the company management, the lead underwriter, the capital markets advisor, the securities counsel, and the auditors. All aspects of the offering need to be discussed.

- Timing of the offering
- Size of the offering
- Target price range for the securities
- Fees and expenses for the IPO
- Lock up period for management and investors
- Use of proceeds

DUE DILIGENCE

Performing due diligence on the company is a critical part of the work that has to be done to ensure that there are no material misstatements or omissions in the registration statement filed by the company. The Securities Act of 1933 requires that all parties involved in the IPO process are held liable for the information published by the company. As a result, the company's underwriter and attorneys will perform a thorough due diligence of the company including interviewing the management and the board, reviewing financials and tax filings, contracts, board meeting minutes, and so on. All parties have to thoroughly review the registration statement to ensure that it is completely accurate and there are no material omissions. Finally, as part of the due diligence process, the underwriter will request a "comfort" letter from the company's independent auditors. Generally, two comfort letters are issued to the underwriters—one at the time the underwriting agreement is signed and one at the closing date.

FILING THE REGISTRATION STATEMENT

Once the registration statement is completed, it is sent to the SEC for review electronically via EDGAR (the Electronic Data Gathering, Analysis, and Retrieval system). Companies are permitted to submit the registration statement to the SEC on a confidential basis. The initial submission and all amendments must be filed no later than fifteen calendar days before the date on which the company conducts a roadshow. Once the statement is submitted, the SEC has thirty days to perform the initial review and provide comments. The statement is reviewed by SEC staff consisting of an accountant, attorney, and financial analyst.

SEC REVIEW AND RESPONSE

After review of the registration statement is completed, the SEC staff typically issues a comment letter that provides questions, possible deficiencies, and suggested revisions. Each individual comment in the staff's letter must be addressed and resolved in writing before the registration statement can become effective. Once revisions to the registration statement are made, an amended registration statement is also filed via EDGAR. After the filing is effective, the comment letters and the company's responses are publicly available via EDGAR. In addition, if there are material changes to the company's business, these must also be reported to the SEC.

THE ROADSHOW

The roadshow is a critical part of a successful IPO. The underwriter will work with the management team to help prepare the company's pitch as well as arrange for meetings with financial analysts and institutional investors. These meetings typically take place over a two-week period and can be grueling. It is expected that the CEO and CFO attend and present the management story. While the company prospectus will be shared with the attendees, it should not be assumed that people have read it in advance of the meeting. It is important that the management team members present their story in a confident and credible manner and adequately address any questions that come up.

PRICING AMENDMENT AND UNDERWRITING AGREEMENT

As the company gets closer to the IPO, it needs to agree with the underwriter on the final price to be set for the company shares. In setting the offering price, the underwriter will look at comparables for other companies in the space and apply earnings, EBITDA (Earnings Before Interest, Taxes, Depreciation, and Amortization, a metric that helps evaluate a company's performance), or cash flow-based multiples. It will also look at the market conditions, how other recent IPOs have done in the market, and an IPO discount so that the company's stock has a nice pop on the day of the IPO. Upon completion of an agreement with the underwriter on the pricing, the final underwriter agreement is signed. Also, at this time, the final amendment to the registration statement is prepared, including the offering price, underwriter's discount or commission, and the net proceeds to the company. This amendment is called the pricing amendment and is filed with the SEC.

THE CLOSING

The closing marks the conclusion of the long IPO process. Typically, the company shares will begin trading the morning after the pricing is finalized. The closing occurs after all the shares have been sold, or the company and the underwriters agree in the case of a "best efforts" scenario that the selling effort is concluded. The closing is a formal meeting that is usually attended by the company and its counsel, the lead underwriter and its counsel, the registrar and transfer agent, and the auditors. The underwriters wire the company the funds for the net proceeds of the offering. The registrar and transfer agent record the stock. The underwriter's counsel provides legal opinions, and the auditors give the underwriters a second comfort letter as of the closing date.

The Smartsheet IPO

Smartsheet is a Seattle-based provider of a cloud native spreadsheet platform that went public on April 27, 2018. According to its S-1, Smartsheet is "a leading cloud-based platform for work execution, enabling teams and organizations to plan, capture, manage, automate, and report on work at scale, resulting in more efficient processes and better business outcomes." For example, Cisco uses Smartsheet to oversee a $300 million annual spend on programs and technology, produce events, manage infrastructure projects, support service engagements, orchestrate marketing campaigns, and manage sale execution. At the time of its IPO, it had 92,000 customers, ninety companies in the Fortune 100, and two-thirds of the companies in the Fortune 500.

I spoke with Matt McIlwain, a managing director at Madrona Venture Group, a top Seattle VC firm and an investor in Smartsheet. He indicated that the board started evaluating the prospect for the company to go public about twelve to eighteen months in advance of the IPO. At the IPO, the company met the two main criteria I had outlined earlier—in other words, more than $100 million in revenues (Smartsheet had reported $110 million in revenues in the most recent fiscal year) and greater than 30 percent yearly revenue growth (they were at 66 percent).

The board also looked at the scalability of the company and the predictability of the revenues to make sure that the company would continue to grow rapidly following the IPO. The company had no issues with scaling its platform and onboarding new customers. The vast majority of the time, the company did not require the involvement of a professional services team, which can often limit the pace at which companies can onboard new customers. The growth potential for the company also looked strong based on a number of different metrics. The company, for example, had more than one hundred thousand new trials in the twelve months prior to the IPO. Another key metric that the board looked at was the net dollar retention (NDR), which measures the growth in year-over-year revenues from each account. In the case of Smartsheet, its NDR was 130 percent, which is considered very good for SaaS-based companies. In fact, this metric was even higher at 149 percent for companies whose annual contract value was greater than $5,000. These two metrics gave the board strong confidence that the growth potential for the company was significant for the foreseeable future. Matt mentioned as a counter example another company in its portfolio, Apptio, which had a lower NDR, much higher involvement of professional services, and significantly lumpier sales when it went public. It's not surprising that Apptio missed its revenue forecast the second quarter after its IPO and its stock price took a significant beating as a result. More on Apptio later in the book.

The company started its investment banker bake-off in the fall of 2017 and evaluated a total of eight investment banks. They selected Morgan Stanley and JPMorgan Chase as its lead bankers, though Goldman Sachs was also in hot contention. At the end of the day, the company felt that its IPO was a bit small for Goldman. The other factor that played into the company's choice was the introduction that these banks had made to institutional investors and how they had positioned the company in these conversations.

The company filed its final S-1 for a $150 million IPO on March 26, 2018, and went public on April 27, 2018. It originally established a price range of $10 to $12, but after receiving strong feedback following its roadshow, it boosted its price range to $12 to $14. It ended up pricing the stock at $15, which popped to $18.40 at its debut, a

22 percent rise over its IPO price. The board was overall very pleased with the pricing of the stock because it felt that the bankers didn't leave much money on the table with its IPO pricing.

The company has continued to grow rapidly and is currently at a $300 million ARR in 2020. One year after the IPO, the company completed a $339 million secondary offering. As of the writing of this book, the stock price has tripled to $47, though it is encountering some headwinds due to the coronavirus pandemic.

Direct Listing

Direct listing is an emerging trend for startups to go public in which companies don't raise money but directly list their stock at one of the stock exchanges. Spotify pioneered this model when it went public on the New York Stock Exchange in 2018. They were followed by Slack, which also pursued this model when it went public in 2019. The most recent direct listing as of the writing of this book was Palantir, which went public on September 30, 2020. In a direct listing, no shares are sold by the company—instead, the insiders (founders, investors, employees) will sell their stock to the public. Spotify, Slack, and Palantir were able to use this approach because they had raised substantial capital in the private markets prior to going public.

Many VCs like Bill Gurley from Benchmark believe that the main benefit of a direct listing is that the stock is not sold at a discount to its true value. According to Bill, there's been more than $171 billion in underpricing of stock in IPOs in the last few decades. Zoom, which had a successful IPO, for example, lost more than $600 million in share value from the pop that they got in their stock price on the day of their IPO. Jay Ritter, an IPO expert and a professor at the University of Florida, suggests that top investment banks like

Goldman Sachs and Morgan Stanley have underpriced their IPOs on the average by 33.5 percent and 29.2 percent, respectively. Investment banks believe that they need to demonstrate a substantial pop in the IPO price to have a successful IPO when, in fact, the money should have rightly gone to the company. The investment banks also have existing relationships with large investors that make the initial purchase commitment, and they feel that they need to sell them the company stock at a discount to gain their commitment and further their relationship with those investors.

Another benefit of the direct listing approach is that the VCs and founders in the startup don't have to enter into a lockup period (typically six months) with the investment banks when they cannot sell their stock. With a direct listing, they can gain liquidity for their stock immediately. Employees can also sell their stock at opening.

Finally, another reason to consider a direct listing is that the fees that you need to pay the investment banks are substantially less when compared to an IPO. With an IPO, the investment banks will typically charge a fee that is 7 percent of the funds raised in the IPO. If you add a typical discount of 18 percent for the stock price (which is the average underpricing), you could end up paying 25 percent or higher with an IPO. The investment banks still, however, earn a substantial amount in a direct listing. For example, Spotify and Slack paid their investment banks $35 million and $22 million, respectively, in advisory fees.

The main disadvantage of a direct listing is that the company doesn't get to control the investors who purchase the stock. The company doesn't get the benefit of selecting well-regarded institutional investors to invest long term in the stock. Instead, a significant portion of the stock may end up in the hands of short sellers who may pressure the stock price. There's also a risk of wild swings in the stock price as the company doesn't control the amount of stock being sold and is reliant on existing investors to sell stock on the day of the direct listing.

The pros and cons of using a direct listing can be summarized as follows:

Pros	Cons
Stock is sold at true market price	Stock price is subject to market supply and demand and potentially significant market swings
Less dilution for existing shareholders	No additional capital raised by the company
Equal access for all buyers and sellers	Inability to control which shareholders get to purchase shares
Lower investment advisory fees	Financial advisors cannot participate in investor meetings
No lockup period. Immediate liquidity for existing shareholders	No traditional IPO roadshow. May make it difficult to attract large institutional investors
Ability to provide forward-looking guidance	

The activities in both an IPO and a direct listing are very similar and include registration, investor education, trading, and so on. The S-1 filing process and review process with the SEC is similar except that with a direct listing the S-1 will become effective one to two weeks prior to the stock going public. This allows the company to publicly announce forward-looking guidance in advance of the stock trading, thus enabling potential investors to more accurately price the stock.

In an IPO, there is traditionally a book-building process with a two-week roadshow to build interest and gain purchase commitments from institutional investors. With a direct listing, investor education is typically done with an Investor Day webcast where anyone can call in to listen to the company's pitch. The webcast is not limited just to institutional investors and is more democratic as a result. This was a key consideration for the founders of Spotify in choosing the direct listing route.

The day before the trading of the stock begins, the stock exchange will declare a reference price for the stock in consultation with the company's investment advisor. Typically, the reference price is the average price for the most recent private trades. On the day of the trading, the direct market maker (DMM) in the stock will determine the buy and sell interest in the stock, and buyers and sellers will adjust their orders as the market begins the process of establishing an equilibrium price. Typically, it will take several hours for the market to settle and for the DMM to open the stock to the broader market.

As of the writing of this book, we are still in the early stages of establishing the direct listing as a viable approach to going public for startups. Most companies are still pursuing a traditional IPO approach since it is considered the "safe" route, and most startup CEOs don't want to take a chance with anything other than a tried and true approach. Many analysts have said that a direct listing can only work at this stage for companies that are well-known brands with an easy-to-understand business model. However, as more companies pursue the direct listing route, this will become less of a requirement. Direct listing is also not an appropriate strategy if you are looking to raise funding when you go public. However, there is no reason that a company cannot do a private offering in advance of going public and use a direct listing approach when going public.

My hope is that the direct listing approach will eventually become a preferred mechanism for going public. Certainly, a number of top-tier VC firms like Benchmark and Andreessen Horowitz are calling for this change. It will significantly reduce the cost for companies to go public and allow them to capture all the gains from the appreciation of their stock price.

SPACs
(Special Purpose Acquisition Companies)

SPACs are "blank check" companies created solely to raise capital through an IPO in order to subsequently merge with private companies. SPACs were first created in the 1990s, but they didn't gain popularity with investors until recently. According to Dealogic, SPACs have raised a record $40 billion in funding in 2020 (compared to $13.6 billion in 2019). SPACs are an alternative way for companies to go public where the funds are first raised in an IPO by experienced investors followed by a merger with the target company. Electric truck startup Nikola and sports-betting operator DraftKings Inc. are among the large firms that have gone public in 2020 through SPAC deals.

SPACs have been raised by a range of individuals—former House of Representative speaker Paul Ryan has a SPAC, as does Oakland Athletics executive Billy Beane and brash Silicon Valley investor Chamath Palihapitiya.

The sponsors of a SPAC go through an IPO process that is very similar to a traditional IPO except that there are no financials to share as there is no operating company. The sponsors typically get a 20 percent stake in the SPAC at a nominal share price. The proceeds raised in the IPO are placed in a trust account while the SPAC's management team seeks to complete an acquisition of an existing operating company, generally in a specific industry. The SPAC sponsors have typically eighteen to twenty-four months (as stated in the SPAC's governing documents) to complete the acquisition. If the SPAC successfully completes an acquisition, the acquired company succeeds to the SPAC's public filing status and, as a result, becomes a public company. If the SPAC is unable to complete an acquisition in the designated time frame, the cash held in its trust account is returned to its investors. The SPAC can extend its timeline via a proxy process. The investors in the SPAC can also vote against the proposed acquisition and get their money back.

A typical de-SPAC process (process of unwinding the SPAC and merging with the target company) involves the following steps:

- Diligence/negotiation—one to two months. A transaction is announced upon completion of the negotiations.
- Registration statement preparation—two to four months. At the end of this period, a merger proxy, which includes a description of the proposed merger, financial information of the target company, historical audited financials, management discussion and analysis, and pro-forma financial statements, is filed.
- SEC comment period and shareholder notice period— two to four months. If an affirmative vote is received from the investors, the acquisition can close by merging into the SPAC. The target company then becomes a publicly traded entity.
- Filing of super 8-K statement—this has to be filed within four days of the transaction closing. It must contain substantially the same information that would be required in a registration statement for companies that go through a traditional IPO.
- Filing of 10-Q and 10-K—10-Q has to be filed within forty-five days and the 10-K within ninety days.

From the perspective of the acquired company, the SPAC process provides a number of benefits:

- It provides the ability for earlier-stage companies to go public. Generally, the companies have lower revenues and less established business models and are still incurring significant losses.

- It provides for greater market certainty on the share price at which the company goes public, especially in volatile market conditions, as the acquisition price is negotiated with the SPAC.
- It provides access to experienced managers from the SPAC who can guide the company in its growth phase after it goes public.

The main challenge for the acquired company is that the company has to be ready to operate as a public company in a four- to five-month period.

Time will tell if SPACs remain a popular investment vehicle in the future. It is likely that the post-IPO performance of the SPAC companies will disappoint investors, as these are typically earlier-stage companies that may lack predictability of revenues. Some of the craze behind the SPACs is because of the investment capital looking for higher returns in an era of low interest rates. As the economy improves and interest rates go higher, investors may choose to invest in less risky assets in the future.

Life as a Public Company

While achieving a successful IPO is a major accomplishment and validation of the founders' vision, it is just the beginning of a critical phase in the company's life. As discussed earlier, the company will face significantly greater scrutiny of its products, financial performance, and legal and regulatory compliance. The company will need to invest in an investor relations department as well as hire an experienced public relations firm to manage its relationships with analysts, its institutional investors, and the investing public at large. The company will be on a much shorter leash to manage its quarterly expectations and performance as any miss will undoubtedly have a major impact on its stock price. In addition, it becomes liable for class action lawsuits and shareholder activism that can cause the company to take short-term actions that are detrimental to its long-term growth.

Public companies are obligated to report their financial performance on a quarterly and annual basis. On a quarterly basis, the company needs to file a 10-Q report for each of the first three quarters of the fiscal year. It includes condensed financial data and information on significant events. In addition, SEC rules require that the interim financial information included in the quarterly report be subject to review by an independent auditor prior to filing. On an annual basis, the company has to file a 10-K report. This report includes detailed information about the company's activities, risks, financial performance, and results of operations. It also contains the company's audited annual financial statements, which include the external auditor's opinion of financial statements and an attestation of the company's internal controls as required by Section 404 of Sarbanes-Oxley.

30

INSPIRING
STARTUP STORIES

Icertis

Icertis is a SaaS contract management company that was founded by Samir Bodas and Monish Darda in 2009. Samir was formerly a veteran of Microsoft and the CEO of Aztecsoft, a mid-Cap IT services company. Monish was a director of product development at BMC software, an enterprise software company. Both of the founders wanted to start a product company but didn't have a clear idea of what product to build. Since they didn't have a product in mind that they wanted to build, they focused initially on providing IT services to enterprise customers. This meant that they had to invest very little in the company as customer contracts paid for hiring the employees they needed. In fact, Icertis was founded with less than a $10,000 investment in the company.

Both of the founders knew that, to be successful, they needed to ride an emerging technology wave and they had to do so early in the cycle. At that time, there were a number of technology waves that were emerging, including social networking, mobile commerce, and the cloud. At that time, Amazon was getting early traction with EC2 and S3 and Microsoft had also started to invest heavily in the cloud. Given their B2B backgrounds, the Icertis founders felt that the best opportunities would present themselves in the cloud. They also felt that the applications that would be first to move to the cloud were at the edge of the enterprise—for example, those applications that dealt with business partners—as there would be less security and privacy concerns.

In late 2010, by happenstance, Samir met the associate legal counsel from Microsoft at a get-together. Samir mentioned that he had started a software company but had not decided on what to build. The Microsoft legal counsel suggested that they build a contract management system. When he heard the suggestion, it didn't make any sense to Samir. After all, all it took to develop a contract was to write the contract in Microsoft Word and file the completed contract in a filing system or a file server. The Microsoft legal counsel explained that the whole process in creating a contract involved a significant amount of workflow—from deciding which clauses to incorporate, to getting the contract approved and signed, to communicating pricing information to the procurement organization, and so on. Fortunately, Samir decided to pursue the idea and eventually secured a contract from Microsoft to build a contract management system on the Azure platform. The contract management category met the criteria that he had established about pursuing categories that were on the edge of the enterprise since most contracts are negotiated with external partners. This would be a perfect application that could be developed natively as a cloud-based application.

The contract management market at that time was relatively small—around $300 million in size. Most of the solutions at that time were client server–based solutions that were either too broad but not enterprise class or deep but very narrow in their focus (i.e., they could only handle a certain class of contracts). Initially, the Icertis team built a contract management system to only handle NDAs as NDAs were the highest-volume category of contracts that Microsoft was handling. However, in developing their system, Icertis did a smart thing by building a generic platform architecture to handle multiple document types with an underlying workflow engine. The contract management system was built as an application on top of this platform. Interestingly, Icertis also built other enterprise apps—a cargo transportation app, a fleet management app, a public transportation app, and a compliance app. At that time, Icertis did not have the confidence that the contract management category would be big and thought that they would have to offer multiple enterprise apps to reach $100 million in revenues.

In 2014, the contract management app took off. They sold to Johnson & Johnson and Airtel and reached $1 million in ARR (annual recurring revenues). At that time, Samir had a fortuitous meeting with Pradeep Singh, also a former Microsoft veteran and successful serial entrepreneur. Pradeep had been Samir's hiring manager at Microsoft and knew him well. When Pradeep found out that Icertis was getting traction with its contract management app, he pressed Samir hard to focus only on selling this app and to get out of the other categories. He made the case that, as a small company, Icertis lacked the resources to invest in adequately building all five applications. In addition, the buyers for these apps in the enterprise would be all different. Finally, Pradeep suggested that the company should raise funding to drive growth for the contract management app. While he was initially skeptical, Samir decided to take Pradeep's advice and went out in the market to raise funding for his company.

I asked Samir about how he made the case to the VCs on "Why now" for the contract management category. He indicated that there were five main reasons:

- The speed of business had increased dramatically, and the competitive environment had intensified significantly for large corporations. Contracts contained information on important business relationships. It was important to digitize the information in contracts so that businesses could properly execute on contractual relationships and partnerships.
- Businesses were experiencing significant regulatory changes across multiple geographies that they needed to be in compliance with while executing on their businesses.
- Companies were hiring more and more millennials who had a do-it-themselves mentality. For example, they would much rather utilize a self-help tool to build their own contract without requiring help from the legal department.
- New technologies like AI/ML were becoming available that could help parse contracts, extract meaning, and turn them into live assets.
- There was increasing imperative to move all enterprise apps to the cloud and contract management being at the edge of the enterprise would be one of the first applications that companies would want to move to the cloud.

Samir got a strong reception from VCs for his pitch. He received three term sheets and raised $6 million in Series A funding from Greycroft and Eight Roads India (Fidelity) at a pre-money valuation of $22.5 million. Subsequently, he raised $15 million in funding in 2016 led by Ignition Ventures, $25 million in funding in 2017 from B Capital, $50 million in funding from Meritech Capital in 2018, and $115 million in funding in 2019 from Premji Invest and Greycroft. In five years, the company has grown from $1 million in ARR to more than $100 million in revenues. The company is the market leader in the contract management category that analysts believe is now more than $20 billion in size.

Snowflake

Snowflake Inc. is a leading cloud-based data-warehousing startup that was founded in 2012. It has raised more than $1.4 billion in venture capital, and is based in San Mateo, California. The idea for Snowflake originated from Mike Spieser, who is a managing director at Sutter Hill Ventures. A key investment approach at Sutter Hill is to look at industries in transition and take successful technologies and remake them in a new world. A key technology that he started looking into was data warehousing technologies. Originally, he thought that data warehousing could be transformed using Flash technologies—however, that hypothesis turned out to be wrong. He spoke with a number of database developers and ran into Benoit Dageville and Thierry Cruanes (Snowflake founders) at Oracle. They indicated that storage was not the issue; CPU was the issue, and data warehousing could be reimagined with CPU on demand in the cloud. They felt that data warehousing could be scaled to a much higher level and a lower cost structure in the cloud. According to Bob Muglia, a former CEO at Snowflake, "Snowflake was made possible at that time by a combination of virtualized compute on demand, perfectly durable blob storage, and fast, cheap broadband networks that provided acceptable response times."

Snowflake raised $1 million in seed funding followed by $5 million in Series A funding from Sutter Hill Ventures in 2012. Bob Muglia, who was a senior executive at Microsoft, joined the company in 2014 as its CEO. Right before Bob joined as CEO, the company raised a $20 million round from Redpoint Ventures though the company was still a year away from shipping their product. For the first year, Bob focused his time on shipping the product, developing the business model, engaging with customers, and hiring a sales team.

Bob developed a unique and clever business model for Snowflake. Unlike AWS, where customers paid for physical resources that were being provisioned such as CPU nodes and storage, Bob developed a business model where these physical resources were abstracted away. With Snowflake, customers paid for a virtual warehouse of a certain size—for example, small, medium, and large. This way, customers couldn't easily compare prices between Snowflake and AWS. In addition to virtualizing the resources, Bob also developed the concept of credits with the idea that credits could be discounted if the customer committed to a certain capacity of data warehouses every year. This allowed the company to develop an ARR (annual recurring revenue) model that made the revenue stream more predictable. The only exception to the virtualized model was storage where Snowflake couldn't get customers to pay any more for storage than the pricing on AWS.

Bob's go-to-market strategy was to hire a field sales organization in various metros in the United States that cold-called potential customers. Fortunately, the company had raised a significant amount of money so they could afford to pursue this strategy. To allay customer concerns, Bob had to also invest in enterprise security and certifications. Their initial beachhead was with organizations that were already in the cloud, which included online media, advertising, and technology companies. Eventually, they gained a strong foothold in retail and healthcare as well. Revenues were slow to pick up for the first few years but accelerated significantly in year 4. The company did a few hundred thousand dollars in revenues in the first year, $1 million in revenues in the second year, $3 million in the third year, and $15 million in the fourth year. Revenues tripled every year thereafter reaching in excess of $200 million in 2020. This kind of revenue trajectory is not unusual for an infrastructure company as technology and markets take time to mature.

Snowflake's main competitor in the cloud is a product called Amazon RedShift. It was a very good product but didn't scale after a certain point. In fact, some of Snowflake's best customers were RedShift customers who switched to Snowflake because they couldn't scale their data warehouse effectively on RedShift. Another competitor is BigQuery from Google, which Snowflake considers to be the number two product in the market. Fortunately for Snowflake, BigQuery is available only on the Google Cloud Platform, which limits its appeal given GCP's small market share in the cloud space. A third emerging competitor is a company called DataBricks, which is in the predictive analytics/ML space. The data warehousing and predictive analytics markets are starting to merge, and DataBricks is increasingly becoming a competitor to Snowflake.

In 2020, Snowflake had more than three thousand customers compared to 1,547 customers in 2019. It has seven customers from the Fortune 10 and 146 from the Fortune 500. Revenues increased from $96.7 million in fiscal year ending 2019 to $264.7 million for an incredible growth rate of 174 percent. The company raised a $479 million round at a $12.4 billion valuation in February 2020. In September 2020, Snowflake successfully executed the largest software IPO in history. The closing price of $254 was triple the original pricing and double the initial pricing of $120 per share. Its valuation reached $70 billion, which was more than five times its valuation in February 2020.[1]

OfferUp

OfferUp is a leading mobile-centric marketplace for used goods headquartered in Bellevue, Washington. It was founded by Nick Huzar and Arean van Veelen in 2009. These were the early days of the smartphone and they were struck by the potential offered by a camera on a smartphone. As they discussed various opportunities to leverage the presence of a camera on a smartphone, they felt that there was a big opportunity for people to use their smartphone to sell their used goods. They organized some garage sales and tried to sell their used items on Craigslist to learn about the experience. They found that the process was anything but easy. Craigslist also had a reputation for not being a safe platform to sell secondhand items. They did some research and came to the realization that Craigslist was addressing only 10 percent of the market and that there was a vast untapped market available for them to pursue. They felt that with a smartphone they could it make significantly easier for people to take pictures of their used items and put them up for sale in their local neighborhood. Messaging between buyers and sellers could be instantaneous, further greasing the path for e-commerce.

The company launched with a basic mobile app and a website under the name DitchThis. However, fundraising was hard as investors wanted to see them generating revenues. As a result, they went through a pivot targeting small businesses where these businesses could publish their deals through their app. However, the pivot did not work and finally in 2011 the company found investors who were excited by their original consumer-focused vision and decided to refocus the company on this vision as OfferUp. Given the ultimate success of OfferUp's consumer vision, it illustrates the importance of sticking to your guns and ignoring the advice of uninformed investors who may not truly understand the market opportunity that you are addressing.

In September 2011, the team built their first C2C app creating a marketplace for users to sell their used items to others in their surrounding neighborhoods. They undertook a number of promotional activities to promote the app in local Seattle festivals such as the Bite of Seattle. They also looked into online advertising to target Seattle-area users—however, none of the existing ad platforms provided precise ad targeting by zip code. As a result, the company had very little traction that year. Finally, their luck turned in January 2013 when Facebook launched a beta of their app install advertising program. They could now target users in specific locations by zip code.

The company decided to initially target users in Bellevue, Washington—a suburb of Seattle. The Facebook ad install program turned out to be very successful for OfferUp, allowing the company to acquire users at only $0.25 per download. They were now able to create a sufficient density of users in a very specific location that would allow a true marketplace to emerge in that location. They also made it very easy for users to post items for sale on OfferUp through a wizard-like process. They found that once someone sold an item on OfferUp, they would come back to post many more items on the platform. This soon created a vibrant marketplace with thousands of items for sale that in turn encouraged new users to post their items for sale. Unlike Craigslist, where people communicated via email, users on OfferUp could communicate with each other instantly with in-app messaging, which allowed sellers to sell their goods more quickly.

While OfferUp was finally starting to get traction, they were also starting to run out of money. One of the founders, Arean van Veelen, came up with the idea for CEO Nick Huzar to send an update with metrics demonstrating their traction to the investors that they had met previously. Fortunately, one of the investors, Sigma West (now Jackson Square Ventures), responded immediately and asked if they could fly down the following Monday to meet with them in person. The meeting went well, especially since Sigma West had a strong experience with marketplaces. Eventually, the firm made a $2.8 million Series A investment in the company.

With the new investment, the company invested in hiring and decided to expand into Tacoma, a neighboring city to Seattle, and into Portland. These expansions went well and it gave the company the confidence that it had found the secret sauce to expand into other markets. On the strength of its success in Seattle-Tacoma and Portland, in 2014, the company expanded into five additional markets and also raised a $15.8 million round from Andreessen Horowitz. The team was particularly excited about having Jeff Jordan, a partner from Andreessen Horowitz, join the board. Jeff brought extensive experience in marketplaces as the former president of eBay, North America. One of the critical decisions that the company took was not to publicize their success as they were afraid that it would spawn competitors in other markets before they had a chance to expand into those markets.

The company grew rapidly into other markets in the United States and became a top shopping app. Until it raised its Series D in November 2016, it had raised all its funding on the merits of its growth with more than $14 billion in transactions being consummated on its marketplace that year. However, it had virtually no revenues until then. Following its Series D, the company finally started working on monetizing its app as it felt that it could no longer find investors who would continue to invest purely on its rapid growth. The company first launched a monetization initiative where users could pay to "bump" their item for sale to a more prominent position in the app. Over time, this feature transformed into a promoted listing feature on the app. It also noticed that a number of car dealers were promoting used cars on its platform. In 2018, it introduced a program for auto dealers to promote their used car inventory on OfferUp for a subscription fee. OfferUp claims that 10 percent of used car sales in the United States happens through its platform. Finally, in 2018, it also introduced a shipment feature where sellers could ship their items to other users in adjacent cities. OfferUp takes a 7.9 percent cut of the transaction.

OfferUp is now a top 50 app on both the iOS and Android App stores with more than 80 million downloads. It claims to have 20 million monthly active users. In Seattle alone, 20 percent of the population actively uses OfferUp to sell and buy used items. In March 2020, the company merged with Letgo—one its main competitors in North America—and took in an additional $130 million in funding from the OLX group. The OLX group, which had a majority stake in Letgo, now owns 40 percent of the combined entity. OfferUp faces strong competition from Craigslist and Facebook but has clearly established itself as a major used goods marketplace in the United States.

Apptio

Apptio, based in Bellevue, Washington, develops technology business management software for mid-size to large enterprises looking for smart ways to manage their IT budget. According its website, "Apptio SaaS solutions help organizations make smart decisions as they analyze, plan, optimize, control, and collaborate about the investments that will transform the IT operating model." The company has referred to itself as the "Quickbooks" of IT spending. The company was founded in 2007 by Sunny Gupta, CEO; along with Kurt Shintaffer, CFO; and Paul McLaughlan, CTO. Prior to Apptio, Sunny was a serial entrepreneur who founded two other companies that had successful exits with Rational and Opsware, respectively.

The idea for Apptio emerged out a chance meeting that Sunny Gupta had with the CIO of Goldman Sachs while he was contemplating his next move after selling his previous company, iConclude. The Goldman CIO told him that they had a big spend on IT at their firm and that ERP systems at that time were inadequate for them to effectively manage their IT spend. Sunny took the idea and interviewed forty IT leaders to validate that this was indeed a real need. After the interviews, Sunny came away convinced that this was a big idea though he felt that it would be hard and complex to execute since he would be creating a brand-new application category.

While it was a real challenge for Sunny to raise funding for his previous company, iConclude, he had a much easier time raising funding for Apptio. Since iConclude had a strong exit, all the investors in Apptio (Greylock, Shasta Ventures, and Madrona Venture Group) decided to invest $7 million at a $15 million valuation before Apptio had written a single line of code. Upon receiving funding, the company worked hard over the next seven months to develop its platform and to acquire five design partners to test its solution. It had its first paying customer in March 2008 and ended that year with about $300,000 to $400,000 in exit ARR. From there revenues grew rapidly to $1.5 million, then to $6 million, $18 million, and $50 million in revenues. Its business model was to charge companies a small percentage of their total IT spend.

Apptio's original business plan was to go after smaller companies as they felt that they didn't have the product maturity and the security capabilities to go after bigger companies. However, the problem that they were addressing was more acute for larger companies. In the 2008–2009 time frame, in the middle of the global financial crisis, the company successfully repositioned itself as a significant cost cutting tool for larger companies. It was able to sign up major customers such as JP Morgan, Bank of America, and Cisco for $1 million+ deals. Today, more than 40 percent of F100 companies are its customers. The company was able to make the transition to large customers as a result of deep customer focus and empathy. It hired enterprise salespeople who were adept at selling to large companies. The company also established a customer advisory board to help it in developing its product strategy.

In 2011, it was approached by some CIOs to form an independent Technology Business Management (TBM) Council that would develop and promote best practices in this space. Despite some initial reservations, the company helped fund an independent nonprofit organization that has more than thirty CIOs on its board and more than ten thousand members.

While the company grew very nicely in its early years, sales started to slow down in the 2013 time frame as it tapped out its early adopters and the company was only able to sell to a select set of large customers. The big challenge that the company faced was that it was not selling into an existing category, and creating a new category was extremely challenging. Getting meetings with CIOs of large companies for a no-name VC-backed company was hard. The decision-making process was also long as it required a company's CFO and CEO to sign off on the purchase. Gartner was unwilling to write about the company as it did not operate in an established category and did not have any real competitors. As a result, the company decided to invest in a lot of money on evangelism and books. Its efforts in establishing the TBM Council also helped in this regard. Finally, it made a real effort sell into smaller companies. To sell into smaller customers, it built applications as opposed to just providing a platform. It reduced delivery timelines from nine months to a few months. Fortunately, the company had raised enough capital to make the kinds of investments necessary to establish the category and expand its customer base.

As revenues started growing again, in 2015, the company decided to pursue an IPO. It felt that it would benefit in a number of ways—employees would finally get liquidity for their shares, it would have the currency to make acquisitions, and it would help from a branding perspective (though that didn't quite turn out to be the case). At the time the company went IPO in 2016, its revenues were $129 million and it was experiencing a growth rate of 21 percent. The company raised $96 million in its IPO. While the stock price popped 46 percent at its IPO, it missed its first earnings expectation and took a major hit to its stock price. It took another six quarters for the stock price to recover. While the overall IPO process was very challenging and time consuming, Sunny Gupta told me that in hindsight he would have still done the IPO, especially since it eventually led to the company's acquisition by Vista Equity Partners.

In 2018, the company encountered more hiccups and the overall market also took a hit, creating significant pressure on its stock price. As a result, the company started getting unsolicited interest from several strategic players. Since the board had a fiduciary responsibility to review the acquisition interest, it hired a banker to evaluate the opportunities. Eventually, Vista Equity Partners came to the table and made an acquisition offer at a 53 percent premium to its then current stock price. The company decided to take the offer as they could operate essentially as an independent company and participate in the upside that it created. Today the company is operating as a fully owned entity under the auspices of Vista Equity and it is likely that the company will make a number of acquisitions before being sold to a larger strategic player in the industry.

UIPath

UIPath is a New York–headquartered global company that is the leader in robotic process automation (RPA) software, which helps companies automate repetitive business processes. The company was founded by Daniel Dines in 2005 in Romania and was originally called DeskOver.

Daniel Dines was the son of a teacher and a civil engineer and grew up behind the Iron Curtain under the communist dictatorship of Nicolae Ceauşescu. He received a master's degree in computer science and math from the University of Bucharest. Daniel learned C++ by borrowing a C++ book from the library and taught himself the language using his friend's computer while he slept. He learned that computer programmers in Romania earned good money doing contracting work for US companies and started doing some consulting work himself. Eventually, he got an offer to join Microsoft in 2001 where he remained until 2005 when he went back to Romania to start DeskOver.

The company originally built software for IT process automation and also did a lot of consulting work to pay the bills. The company struggled for a long time until 2014, when an Indian BPO (Business Process Outsourcing) company came to them looking for software tools to automate routine tasks such as data entry. They were using a competitor's product at that time but found the tools to be too inflexible. This customer interaction opened up Daniel's eyes to the much bigger opportunity to go after the business process automation market.

The company took about six months to deliver an early version of its RPA software to the Indian company and won the contract from its competitor, Blue Prism, which had originally created the category. They started working on a full-fledged version of its software, which took another three years to complete and reach full maturity. The company raised a $1.6 million seed round in July 2015. Being based out of Romania at that time, it was not easy for the company to raise funding. Daniel spoke to only one investment firm and took almost nine months to negotiate the term sheet. The original terms of the term sheet were quite onerous—however, Daniel stuck to his guns, which was made possible because his revenues were growing. In fact, according to Daniel, the investor took common stock in the company (which is very unusual for an investor) and Daniel was able to negotiate a dual class structure for the stock, which he has been able to maintain so far.

With a new focus on RPA, the company invested heavily in global sales and partnerships with consulting companies. Revenues grew very rapidly from $1 million in 2015 to $30 million in 2017, $150 million in 2018, and $300 million in 2019. With fast-growing revenues, the company was able to raise almost $1 billion in funding with the last round being done at a $7 billion valuation. Daniel attributes their success with revenue growth to a number of factors.

- **Focus on sales:** Unlike most technical founders who typically don't have a high opinion of salespeople, Daniel was passionate about sales from the get-go. He spent a significant amount of time on the road traveling internationally helping his sales organization sell their product. Also, unlike his main competitor, Daniel also established his own sales organization as opposed to relying exclusively on consulting firms like Deloitte to drive their sales.

- **Customer-centric product development:** Daniel is a big believer in talking to customers and understanding their requirements. He feels very strongly that customer requirements should drive product development and not the other way around. Because he was an engineer, he felt that he could be tough on the engineering team and push them to develop the product based on customer requirements.

- **Global approach from the start:** Unlike most US companies that start with a US-centric focus and then slowly enter other markets, Daniel was fortunate that the company was originally based in Romania where there was no market. Right from the start, Daniel set out to create a global sales organization. He was the first to expand into India where there were a lot of BPO organizations. He established an early presence in Japan, which today makes up 15 percent of its overall sales. Today the company has offices in Bangalore; New York; Washington, DC; London; and Tokyo.

- **Hybrid on-prem/cloud approach:** Unlike many enterprise software companies that were choosing to go down an exclusively cloud-based approach, UIPath has been agnostic about where the customer would like to utilize its software. The company is able to deliver its software for on-prem installation, on a company-managed cloud environment, or in the public cloud. The company feels that a lot of its customers, especially banks, are very circumspect about allowing their sensitive customer data to leave the premises.

- **Focus on culture:** Daniel is a big believer in the importance of company culture driving the performance of the company. He was deeply influenced by the company culture established by Netflix and spent a lot of time in developing their company culture. Some of the attributes of the company culture include trust, transparency, open technology, and so on. However, Daniel wanted to find one unifying theme that would encompass all the attributes that he wanted to promote. He finally settled on "Being Humble" as the overarching theme for the company. For him that means listening to others, being aware of the market, making faster decisions without losing face, and so on. To reinforce this culture, the company has established an anonymous feedback channel that anyone can use to pinpoint issues. Daniel himself spends time reviewing the feedback on this channel and takes the time to go deep on certain issues that surface.

UIPath successfully navigated the challenges posed by the COVID-19 crisis. The company's revenue grew 81 percent in 2020 to $607.6 million, while losses had shrunk to $92.4 million from $519.9 million in 2019. UiPath had nearly eight thousand customers as of January 31, 2021, including 61 percent of the Fortune Global 500. The company had one of the largest IPOs for a software company, raising $1.3 billion as it debuted on the New York Stock Exchange in April 2021. Shares rose 17 percent when the market opened, valuing the company at $34 billion. The future looks very bright for UIPath as companies look to Robotic Process Automation to automate many work processes and become more efficient.

CONCLUSION

I HAVE HAD THE GOOD fortune of spending fifteen years as an entrepreneur and starting three different companies. It has been an amazing time, especially since I got to make new friends and work with some great people. In particular I am extremely fortunate to have found my cofounders, Shaibal Roy, Krishnan Seshadrinathan, and Raghav Kher, who were not only super-smart people but great human beings as well. I was fortunate to have been mentored by some terrific board members like Sam Jadallah and Pete Higgins during this journey. I am also grateful for the time I spent at Microsoft where I got to learn from the best and contribute to many industry-changing events.

There are many important lessons I have learned through my journey as an entrepreneur. One of the most important lessons is the importance of establishing product/market fit for your startup idea. Without product/market fit, you don't have a company, no matter how much money you are able to raise. Sometimes, you are just eager to jump into launching your product or service without doing the proper due diligence on your idea. But I can tell you from experience that you should take the time to first establish whether you have a viable idea or not.

The founding team is equally important to your success. You need to find a cofounder who is not only a functional expert but also can contribute to the overall product and business strategy of the company. I was extremely lucky that my two cofounders, Shaibal and Krishnan, who came from a technical background, had amazing customer and business instincts despite having no formal business education. They were invaluable to me in brainstorming about our company's strategy as we navigated through many challenges in our startup journey.

Finally, many founders simply focus on the product and neglect thinking through a sound go-to-market strategy to get the word out about their product and acquire customers. With Livemocha, we achieved product/market fit from the get-go but we also had a great marketing team that successfully spread the message about Livemocha to more than 15 million consumers in two hundred different countries. It took great PR, a concerted SEO effort, and a clever SEM strategy to achieve this level of success.

I remain passionate about helping other entrepreneurs realize their entrepreneurial dreams and will continue to write about entrepreneurship on this book's website (http://www.startuptoexitbook.com/) and on LinkedIn (https://www.linkedin.com/in/shirishn/) and Twitter (@Shirishn). I hope that you will follow me on LinkedIn and Twitter and contribute to my ongoing conversation on entrepreneurship.

GOOD LUCK!

ACKNOWLEDGMENTS

I AM VERY GRATEFUL FOR the tremendous amount of help I received for the book from my friends and colleagues. My manuscript received an extensive amount of review from my former legal counsel, Craig Sherman from Wilson Sonsini Goodrich & Rosati. His review of the company formation and financing sections was invaluable in making sure that I had correctly characterized all the legal aspects involved. I also received help from Duncan Butcher, a partner at Miller Nash Graham and Dunn in reviewing the Company Formation section. Completing the legal review was Rajiv Sarathy, a partner at Perkins Coie, who reviewed the patent section to make sure that I had covered the topic accurately. Any errors in these sections are entirely mine.

I am also grateful to my friends and former colleagues—S. Somasegar (managing director at Madrona Venture Group); my cofounders, Krishnan Sesadrinathan and Raghav Kher; longtime friends Phani Vaddadi and Chandan Chauhan (ex-Microsoft alumni); my fellow TiE Seattle board member Satbir Khanuja; and budding entrepreneur Preeti Suri—all of whom reviewed the manuscript and provided invaluable feedback.

Finally, I am grateful to a number of individuals who took the time to do interviews for the book and provide valuable insights about their companies/firms and various aspects of the startup journey. These include Samir Bodas, CEO of Icertis; Sunny Gupta, CEO of Apptio; Bob Muglia, former CEO of Snowflake; Arean van Veelen, founder of OfferUp; Daniel Dines, CEO of UIPath; Matt McIlwain, managing director of Madrona Ventures; and Kevin Cable, managing director at Cascadia Capital.

GLOSSARY OF TERMS

409A Valuation: A 409A valuation is an independent appraisal of the fair market value (FMV) of a private company's common stock. Once a 409A valuation is completed, the company can issue stock options with an exercise price equal to the common stock share price determined by the 409A valuation.

Accelerator: An entity that provides mentorship and funding to startups to help them grow faster and achieve product market fit.

Accredited Investor: An accredited investor is an individual or a business entity, by virtue of their assets or income, as defined by securities law, that is allowed to trade securities that may not be registered with financial authorities.

Angel Investor: An independent wealthy individual who makes an investment in a company with their own money.

Anti-Dilution Protection: An anti-dilution provision is a clause that protects an investor from a reduction in the value of his or her shares due to the issuance by the company of additional shares to other investors at a per share price that is lower than the per share price paid by the investor.

ARR (Annual Recurring Revenue): ARR is a metric for SaaS or subscription businesses with a subscription revenue model. ARR is the value of the contracted recurring revenue that the company expects to receive on an annual basis.

B2B (Business to Business): A B2B business is one that sells primarily to business entities.

B2C (Business to Consumer): A B2C business is one that sells primarily to consumers.

CAC (Customer Acquisition Cost): CAC is a metric that measures the average cost of acquiring a single customer. Typically, the CAC is evaluated in conjunction with the LTV (Customer Lifetime Value). Investors typically like to see a 3:1 ratio or higher of LTV to CAC.

CAP Table (Capitalization Table): A cap table is an accounting of all the equity held by various investors in a company. Investors will typically ask for the company's cap table prior to making an investment.

Convertible Note: A convertible note is a form of short-term debt in a company that automatically converts to equity upon the completion of a qualified financing.

CPC (Cost per Click): Cost per click (CPC) refers to the price you pay for each click in a pay-per-click (PPC) marketing campaign.

CPM (Cost per Mille): CPM is the cost of advertising for a thousand impressions of your advertising creative.

Crowdfunding: A type of funding where a company raises funds from individual unaccredited investors by selling early access to its products or services.

Down Round: A financing where the per share price offered to investors is lower than the previous round of financing.

Due Diligence: An intensive exploration that investors engage in to better understand the company's product offering, go-to-market strategy, financials, and legal obligations in the context of a financing.

Founder's Stock: The common stock issued to founders, typically at a very low par value, during the formation of the company.

Fully Diluted: A calculation that takes into account all shares held by employees and investors along with granted options, available option pool, and warrants. An entity's ownership of a company is always calculated on a fully diluted basis.

IPO (Initial Public Offering): An IPO is the first fund raise by a company where the stock of the company is offered for sale to the general public.

Lead Investor: An investor who leads a financing on behalf of all investors and sets the terms of the financing.

Liquidation Preference: A right held by investors to receive their funds back before common shareholders in the event of a liquidation or liquidity event.

LTV (Lifetime Value): LTV is the sum of all profits generated by a single customer over the life of the customer's relationship with the company. Typically, the LTV is evaluated in conjunction with the

CAC (Customer Acquisition Cost). Investors typically like to see a 3:1 ratio or higher of LTV to CAC.

MVP (Minimum Viable Product): A minimum viable product is a version of a product with the least number of features to be usable by early customers who can then provide feedback for future product development.

Network Effect: A network effect is a phenomenon by which a product or service gains additional utility as it acquires more users. Facebook is an example of a service that became more valuable to users as more users joined the service.

Option Pool: An option pool is the number of options that have been set aside by a company to award to employees and contractors of the company.

Post-Money Valuation: The post-money valuation is the valuation of the company after an investment has been made in the company.

Preferred Round: A preferred round is an investment round in a company where preferred shares are issued to investors. Preferred shares typically have rights that are superior to common shares.

Pre-Money Valuation: The pre-money valuation is the valuation of a company prior to an investment in the company.

Pro rata: A right that investors have to invest in a future round in proportion to their current ownership in the company.

SAFE (Simple Agreement for Future Equity): A SAFE is an agreement between an investor and a company that provides rights to the investor for future equity in the company. The SAFE investor receives the future shares when a priced round of investment or liquidity event occurs.

Seed Round: A seed round is an investment in a company prior to a Series A investment in the company. Typically, a company raises between $500,000 and $3 million in a seed round.

SEM (Search Engine Marketing): Search engine marketing (SEM) is a form of internet marketing that involves the promotion of websites by increasing their visibility in search engine results pages primarily through paid advertising.

SEO (Search Engine Optimization): Search engine optimization (SEO) is the process of improving the quality and quantity of website traffic to a website or a web page from search engines.

Series A Round: A Series A round is the first major institutional round in the company. A Series A round is typically $3 million or higher in funding.

Series Seed: Series Seed is a form of equity in a company that utilizes a simpler set of investment documentation that was originally created by Fenwick and West. The cost of completing a Series Seed investment is typically significantly less compared to an equity round with a complete set of investment documentation.

Term Sheet: A term sheet is a nonbinding memorandum of understanding between an investor and a company outlining the material terms of the investment in the company.

Valuation Cap: The maximum valuation that investors will invest in a company in a future financing, typically in the context of a convertible note.

Venture Debt: Venture debt is a type of debt financing provided to venture-backed companies by specialized banks or non-bank lenders such as venture debt firms.

Warrant: A warrant is an instrument that offers the holder of the warrant the option to purchase equity in the company at a fixed share price.

APPENDIX

[NEWCO, INC.]
MEMORANDUM OF TERMS

Except with respect to the provisions entitled "**Exclusive negotiations**" and "**Confidentiality**," which are intended to be, and are, legally binding agreements among the parties hereto, this Memorandum of Terms represents only the current thinking of the parties with respect to certain of the major issues relating to the proposed private offering and does not constitute a legally binding agreement. This Memorandum of Terms does not constitute an offer to sell or a solicitation of an offer to buy securities in any state where the offer or sale is not permitted.

THE OFFERING

Issuer: [NewCo, Inc.], a Delaware corporation (the "**Company**")

Securities: Series A Preferred Stock (the "**Preferred**")

Valuation of the Company: $[_____] pre-money

Amount of the offering: $[_____]

Number of shares: [_____] shares

Price per share: $[_____]

Investor(s): [_____] or its affiliated entities (the lead investor(s)), [_____] and other investors acceptable to the Company.

Capitalization: See **Exhibit A** for the prefinancing capitalization of the Company and the *pro forma* capitalization following the proposed offering.

Anticipated closing date: Initial closing on or before [_____], with one or more additional closings within [60] days thereafter.

TERMS OF THE PREFERRED

Dividends: Noncumulative dividends at an annual rate of 8 percent of the purchase price per share in preference to the common stock, when and if declared by the board. Any dividends in excess of the preference will be paid to the common stock.

Liquidation preference: In the event of a liquidation, dissolution or winding up of the Company, the Preferred will have the right to receive the original purchase price plus any declared but unpaid dividends prior to any distribution to the common stock. The remaining assets will be distributed *pro rata* to the holders of common stock on an as-converted basis. A sale of all or substantially all of the Company's assets or a merger or consolidation of the

Company with any other company will be treated as a liquidation of the Company.

Redemption: The Preferred will not have redemption rights.

Conversion: The Preferred may be converted at any time, at the option of the holder, into shares of common stock. The conversion rate will initially be 1:1, subject to anti-dilution and other customary adjustments.

Automatic conversion: Each share of Preferred will automatically convert into common stock, at the then applicable conversion rate, upon (i) the closing of a firmly underwritten public offering of common stock at a price per share that is at least five times the purchase price of the Preferred with gross offering proceeds in excess of $35 million (a "**Qualified Public Offering**"), or (ii) the consent of the holders of at least 50 percent of the then *outstanding shares of Preferred.*

Anti-dilution: The conversion price of the Preferred (which will initially equal the purchase price of the Preferred) will be subject to adjustment, on a broad-based weighted average basis, if the Company issues additional securities at a price per share less than the then applicable conversion price.

There will be no adjustment to the conversion price for issuances of (i) shares issued upon conversion of the Preferred; (ii) shares or options, warrants or other rights issued to employees, consultants or directors in accordance with plans, agreements or similar arrangements; (iii) shares issued upon exercise of options, warrants or convertible securities existing on the closing date; (iv) shares issued as a dividend or distribution on Preferred or for which adjustment is otherwise made pursuant to the certificate of incorporation (e.g., stock splits); (v) shares issued in connection with a registered public offering; (vi) shares issued or issuable pursuant to an acquisition of another corporation or a joint venture agreement approved by the board; (vii) shares issued or issuable to banks, equipment lessors or other financial institutions pursuant to debt financing or commercial transactions approved by the board; (viii) shares issued or issuable in connection with any settlement approved by the board; (ix) shares issued or issuable in connection with sponsored research, collaboration, technology license, development, OEM, marketing or other similar arrangements or strategic partnerships approved by the board; (x) shares issued to suppliers of goods or services in connection with the provision of goods or services pursuant to transactions approved by the board; or (xi) shares that are otherwise excluded by consent of holders of a majority of the Preferred.

General voting rights: Each share of Preferred will have the right to a number of votes equal to the number of shares of common stock issuable upon conversion of each such share of Preferred. The Preferred will vote with the common stock on all matters except as specifically provided herein or as otherwise required by law.

Voting for directors: So long as 25 percent of the originally issued Preferred is outstanding, the holders of Preferred will be entitled to elect one director. The holders of common stock will be entitled to elect two directors. The directors will be entitled to customary indemnification from the Company and reimbursement of reasonable costs of attendance at board meetings.

Protective provisions: So long as at least 10 percent of the originally issued Preferred is outstanding, consent of the holders of at least 50 percent of the Preferred will be required for any action that (i) alters any provision of the certificate of incorporation or the bylaws if it would adversely alter the rights, preferences, privileges or powers of or restrictions on the preferred stock or any series of preferred; (ii) changes the authorized number of shares of preferred stock or any series of preferred; (iii) authorizes or creates any new class or series of shares having rights, preferences or privileges with respect to dividends or liquidation senior to or on a parity with the Preferred or having voting rights other than those granted to the preferred stock generally; (iv) approves any merger, sale of assets or other corporate reorganization or acquisition; (v) approves the purchase, redemption or other acquisition of any common stock of the Company, other than repurchases pursuant to stock restriction agreements approved by the board upon termination of a consultant, director or employee; (vi) declares or pays any dividend or distribution with respect to the common stock; (vii) approves the liquidation or dissolution of the Company; (viii) increases the size of the board; (ix) encumbers or grants a security interest in all or substantially all of the assets of the Company in connection with an indebtedness of the Company; (x) acquires a material amount of assets through a merger or purchase of all or substantially all of the assets or capital stock of another entity; or (xi) increases the number of shares authorized for issuance under any existing stock or option plan or creates any new stock or option plan.

INVESTOR RIGHTS

Information rights: The Company will deliver to each holder of at least [500,000] shares of Preferred, (i) audited annual financial statements within 135 days following year-end, (ii) unaudited quarterly financial statements within 45 days following quarter-end, (iii) unaudited monthly financial statements within 30 days of month-end, and (iv) annual business plans. The information rights will terminate upon an initial public offering.

Registration rights: *Registrable securities.* The common stock issued or issuable upon conversion of the Preferred will be "**Registrable Securities.**"

Demand registration. Subject to customary exceptions, holders of at least 50 percent of the Registrable Securities will be entitled to demand that the Company effect up to two registrations (provided that each such registration has an offering price of at least $10.00 per share with aggregate proceeds of at least $20 million) at any time following the earlier of (i) five years following the closing of the financing and (ii) 180 days following the Company's initial public offering. The Company will have the right to delay such registration under certain circumstances for up to two periods of up to 90 days each in any twelve month period.

"Piggyback" registration. The holders of Registrable Securities will be entitled to "piggyback" registration rights on any registered offering by the Company on its own behalf or on behalf of selling stockholders, subject to customary exceptions. In an underwritten offering, the managing underwriters will have the right, in the event of marketing limitations, to limit the number of Registrable Securities included in the offering, provided that, in an offering other than the initial public offering, the Registrable Securities may not be limited to less than 25 percent of the total offering. In the event of such marketing limitations, each holder of Registrable Securities will have the right to include shares on a *pro rata* basis as among all such holders and to include shares in preference to any other holders of common stock.

S-3 rights. Subject to customary exceptions, holders of Registrable Securities will be entitled to an unlimited number of demand registrations on Form S-3 (if available to the Company) so long as those registered offerings are each for common stock having an aggregate offering price of not less than $1 million. The Company will not be required to file more than two such Form S-3 registration statements in any twelve month period.

Expenses. Subject to customary exceptions, the Company will bear the registration expenses (exclusive of underwriting discounts and commissions) of all demand, piggyback and S-3 registrations, provided that the Company will not be required to pay the fees of more than one counsel to all holders of Registrable Securities.

Termination. The registration rights of a holder of Registrable Securities will terminate on the earlier of (i) such date, on or after the Company's initial public offering, on which such holder may immediately sell all shares of its Registrable Securities under Rule 144 during any 90-day period and (ii) three years after the initial public offering.

Market stand-off. Holders of Registrable Securities will agree not to effect any transactions with respect to any of the Company's securities within 180 days following the Company's initial public offering, provided that all officers, directors and 1 percent stockholders of the Company are similarly bound.

Other provisions. The Investor Rights Agreement will contain such other provisions with respect to registration rights as are customary, including with respect to indemnification, underwriting arrangements and restrictions on the grant of future registration rights.

Right to maintain proportionate ownership: Each holder of at least [500,000] shares of Preferred will have a right to purchase its *pro rata* share of any offering of new securities by the Company, subject to customary exceptions. The *pro rata* share will be based on the ratio of (x) the number of shares of Preferred held by such holder (on an as-converted basis) to (y) the Company's outstanding shares, options and warrants (on an as-converted basis). Participating holders will have the right to purchase, on a *pro rata* basis, any shares as to which eligible holders do not exercise their rights. This right will terminate immediately prior to the Company's initial public offering.

Right of first refusal and co-sale agreement: In the event any founder proposes to transfer any Company shares, the Company will have a right of first refusal to purchase the shares on the same terms as the proposed transfer.

If the Company does not exercise its right of first refusal, holders of Preferred will have a right of first refusal (on a *pro rata* basis among holders of Preferred) with respect to the proposed transfer. Rights to purchase any unsubscribed shares will be reallocated *pro rata* among the other eligible holders of Preferred.

To the extent the rights of first refusal are not exercised, the holders of Preferred will have the right to participate in the proposed transfer on a *pro rata* basis (as among the transferee and the holders of Preferred).

The rights of first refusal and co-sale rights will be subject to customary exceptions and will terminate on an initial public offering.

"Drag-along" right: Subject to customary exceptions, if holders of 50 percent of the Preferred and 50 percent of the common stock approve a proposed sale of the Company to a third party (whether structured as a merger, reorganization, asset sale or otherwise), each stockholder will agree to approve the proposed sale. This right will terminate upon a Qualified Public Offering.

EMPLOYEE MATTERS

Vesting of employee shares: Subject to the discretion of the board, shares and options issued to employees, directors and consultants will be subject to four-year vesting, with 25 percent vesting on the first anniversary of the commencement of services and the remainder vesting monthly thereafter. The Company will have the right, upon termination of services, to repurchase any unvested shares.

Proprietary information agreements: The company will have all employees and consultants into proprietary information and inventions agreements in a form reasonably satisfactory to the investors.

"Key person" life insurance: The company will obtain a "key person" life insurance policy on the founders in the amount of $2 million, with proceeds payable to the company.

Other Matters

Legal fees and expenses: At closing, the company will pay the reasonable fees and expenses of a single counsel to the investors up to a maximum of $35,000.

Exclusive negotiations: From the date of the execution of this Memorandum of Terms until the earlier of (i) [_____], (ii) notice of termination of negotiations by the lead investor(s) and (iii) the initial closing of the financing contemplated by this Memorandum of Terms, neither the Company nor any of its directors, officers, employees or agents will solicit, or participate in negotiations or discussions with respect to, any other investment in, or acquisition of, the Company without the prior consent of the lead investor(s).

Confidentiality: Until the initial closing of the financing contemplated by this Memorandum of Terms, the existence and terms of this Memorandum of Terms shall not be disclosed to any third party without the consent of the Company and the lead investor(s), except as may be (i) reasonably required to consummate the transactions contemplated hereby or (ii) required by law.

Conditions precedent: The investment will be subject to customary conditions, including but not limited to:

- Completion of due diligence to the satisfaction of the investors;
- Negotiation and execution of definitive agreements customary in transactions of this nature;
- Receipt of all required authorizations, approvals and consents;
- Delivery of customary closing certificates and an opinion of counsel for the Company; and
- The absence of material adverse changes with respect to the Company.

ENDNOTES

PREFACE

1. Brad Feld and Jason Mendelson, *Venture Deals: Be Smarter Than Your Lawyer and Venture Capitalist* (Hoboken, N.J.: John Wiley & Sons, 2016).
2. Dan Shapiro, *Hot Seat: The Startup CEO Guidebook* (New York: O'Reilly Media, 2015).

CHAPTER 2

1. Marc Andreessen, "Part 4: The Only Thing That Matters," The PMARCA Guide to Startups, June 25, 2007, https://pmarchive.com/guide_to_startups_part4.html.

CHAPTER 3

1. MG Siegler, "A Pivotal Pivot," Tech Crunch, November 8, 2010, https://techcrunch.com/2010/11/08/instagram-a-pivotal-pivot/?guccounter=1.

CHAPTER 8

1. The Founder Institute provides a FAST (founder/advisor standard template) Agreement at https://fi.co/fast.

CHAPTER 11

1. Team Sequoia, "Writing a Business Plan," Sequoia Capital, https://www.sequoiacap.com/article/writing-a-business-plan/.
2. Pitch deck, Air Bed & Breakfast, https://www.slideshare.net/PitchDeckCoach/airbnb-first-pitch-deck-editable.
3. LinkedIn, "LinkedIn's Series B Pitch to Greyloch," https://www.reidhoffman.org/linkedin-pitch-to-greylock/.
4. Chris Janz, *Point Nine Capital*, Blog, "The Angel VC," March 23, 2016, http://christophjanz.blogspot.com/2016/03/saas-financial-plan-20.html.

CHAPTER 14

1. For more information, see the Y Combinator website, https://www.ycombinator.com/documents/.

CHAPTER 15

1. Ted Wang, Series Seed, Fenwick & West, February 25, 2014, https://www.seriesseed.com.

CHAPTER 16

1. National Venture Capitalist Association, "Model Legal Documents," https://nvca.org/model-legal-documents/.

CHAPTER 21

1. First Round Review, "80% of Your Culture Is Your Founder" (interview with Molly Graham; no date), https://firstround.com/review/80-of-Your-Culture-is-Your-Founder/.
2. Amazon, "Leadership Principles," https://www.amazon.jobs/en/principles.
3. Personal conversation with Samir Bodas, founder and CEO of Icertis.

CHAPTER 23

1. Sequoia Capital, "Prepare a Board Deck," https://www.sequoiacap
.com/article/preparing-a-board-deck/.

CHAPTER 26

1. The costs discussed in this section are as of the writing of this book
(2020). These costs will change over time.

CHAPTER 28

1. Issie Lapowsky, "$243 Million: Crunchbase's Very Rosy Picture of the
Average Startup's Exit," *Inc.*, February 6, 2020, https://www.inc.com
/issie-lapowsky/average-successful-startup-exit.html.
2. Amy Barrett, "Is the IPO Party Over?" *Inc.*, September 12, 2012,
https://www.inc.com/amy-barrett/is-the-ipo-party-over.html?icid
=hmhero.

CHAPTER 30

1. This information came from Snowflake's S-1. See https://www.sec
.gov/Archives/edgar/data/1640147/000162828020013010/
snowflakes-1.htm.

INDEX

ABOUT THE AUTHOR

SHIRISH NADKARNI is a serial entrepreneur with proven success in creating multiple consumer businesses that have scaled to tens of millions of users worldwide. Shirish was the cofounder of Livemocha, the world's largest language learning site with more than fifteen million registered members from more than two hundred countries. Livemocha was acquired by RosettaStone in 2013. Prior to Livemocha, Shirish was the founder of TeamOn Systems, a mobile wireless email pioneer that was acquired by Research in Motion in 2002. The TeamOn technology served as the core foundation for BlackBerry Internet Email, which serviced more than fifty million BlackBerry users.

Shirish received his MBA from Harvard Business School and a BSE in Electrical Engineering from the University of Michigan.